THE BUSINESS HANDBOOK

A Guide to Building Your Own Successful Amway Business

Dexter Yager

©Copyright May, 1985
by Dexter R. Yager, Sr.
Published by
Freedom Distributing Company, Inc.
Pineville, N.C.
Printed in United States of America
ISBN 0-9328-77-06-0

First Printing: May 1985 (25m)
Second Printing: 1986 (25m)
Third Printing: 1987 (25m)
Fourth Printing: 1988 (25m)
Fifth Printing: 1988 (50m)

Dedication

This book is dedicated to you and your future. I believe that with the information you now have in your hands, you can achieve your highest dreams. Success can be yours through uncommon dedication to and consistent pursuit of the high goals of personal liberty and preservation of the American free enterprise system; by replacing the word "try" with the winner's creed, "It shall be done!". Remember: You can do it!

"Don't let anybody steal your dream!"
Build yourself a *SUCCESSFUL AMWAY BUSINESS!*

Acknowledgements

I want to thank all those who have encouraged and/or applauded my putting the knowledge I have gained and developed into writing, combined in one text, for the benefit of others.

I extend my appreciation to two individuals first. One who has greatly aided me in transforming my thoughts and message to paper and therefore making this book eminently more readable than it otherwise might have been—Darryl Hicks. And to one who has helped make this book more easily understood with his illustrative excellence—Burt Mader. Both are professionals in their fields; combining with that their insight as distributors has aided the success of this book.

I am indebted to my son Doyle for adopting this book as his own. He has put extraordinary hours and matchless effort and care into both its creative and literary development. His commitment in writing, rewriting, researching, organizing and editing will give this book the success it so deserves.

I would also like to thank the additional staff members for their help in the preparation of the manuscript and design work.

Cover photography by Dennis Nodine, Charlotte, North Carolina.
Illustrations by Burt Mader, Sudbury, Massachusetts.

Contents

Author's Preface 1

Chapter One　　Blueprints 5

Chapter Two　　Foundations 15

Chapter Three　Dreambuilding 49

Chapter Four　　The Geometric Multi-Level Progression ... 65

Chapter Five　　Building Blocks 73

Chapter Six　　Construction 101

Chapter Seven　Additions 115

Chapter Eight　Cement 121

Chapter Nine　　Better Buildings 135

Chapter Ten　　New Horizons 143

"About the Author"

Dexter Yager is not just another Horatio Alger story. His name is well known to hundreds of thousands of business people throughout the world. As a popular speaker and motivator/dreamer, he spends a great deal of time addressing conventions both in the United States and abroad. He is also the sponsor and host of several large "Free Enterprise Day Celebrations," having a personal commitment to re-establish in the hearts and minds of all people the traditional values upon which the foundation of America was built. He and his wife, Birdie, have attained the level of Crown Direct Distributor in the Amway business. Being the father of seven children and having several grandchildren, Dexter realizes the importance of teaching those principles which makes America great for everyone, regardless of age, race, sex or nationality.

Yager is synonymous with "success," as this Christian businessman has greatly aided in or been responsible for the development of businesses including one of the world's largest convention travel agencies, a bank, a classic group of restaurants, plus a prestigious midwestern hotel and a beautiful racquet club resort in Southern Florida. He is also responsible for a long list of family owned businesses.

He is an author whose books have sold in the millions, one of which includes *Don't Let Anybody Steal Your Dream*, which has sold close to one million copies alone.

To his critics he is naive, simplistic, and shallow; but to the millionaire business people, International bankers and entertainment celebrities who are among his devotees, he is one of a handful of motivators whose achievements are equal to his advice. When the subject is *how to make money*, some men speak more eloquently and cleverly than Dexter Yager, but none you can relate to more; and when it comes to *having money* or *attaining wealth* you will not be able to name many with a style such as his. To use his own terminology, Dexter Yager is a "doer".

AUTHOR'S PREFACE

Without a doubt, the most exciting and successful trend in today's business world is a concept called either "multi-level marketing" or "network marketing."

Informed people of the eighties no longer shun *true* MLM's (as they are sometimes labeled) as illegal pyramids or chain letter—variety schemes; instead, more and more enlightened free-enterprise entrepreneurs are optioning for this ingenius concept as an opportunity to own a profitable, booming business with little risk or initial investment. In fact, *U.S. News and World Report* states in its July 4, 1983 issue that there were 638,000 millionaires in the U.S.* at that time, many of whom made their fortunes through multi-level marketing. I assume there are reasonably many more now.

Business Connections states in its January, 1984 issue that 20 percent of the millionaires in the U.S. have made their fortunes since 1978 in multi-level marketing. According to that same source, MLM is being taught in such prestigious institutions as the Harvard Business School. It also makes reference to statements of both Stanford Research and the *Wall Street Journal*, "that between 50 percent and 65 percent of all goods and services will be sold through multi-level methods by the 1990's."

---

*Presently there are approximately 1.4 million millionaires in the U.S.

1

YOUR PART

By picking up this book with such an obvious title, you have at least shown an interest in the cadillac of all multi-levels. By all comparisons, Amway is the proven leader in the MLM explosion (though I must admit that my remarks are somewhat biased, having received checks from Amway for over 2 decades!).

Let me congratulate you, whether you are merely considering a future as an Amway distributor, or if you are already building a successful Amway business.

Your life is about to change—for the better! It is my desire that this book help you speed up your success process. By applying the principles illustrated throughout this book, you will learn from the mistakes *and* triumphs of those who have blazed the trail ahead of you. What you do with the lessons can revolutionize your life and that of your loved ones. They show you how to apply what you are learning to achieve a life filled with happiness, accomplishment and success.

BUILDING

The vast majority of people have absolutely no idea how to begin to make their dreams come true. You undoubtedly already have all the potential necessary to build your own business, but what good is it . . . if you don't know how to use it? And how can you build a life worth living without any plans or blueprints?

By making your first move to become an Amway distributor, you have started your own success-journey. You may not know all the steps to building your own Amway business and making your dreams come true.

However, by using this knowledge and adding fuel to it by exercising your right to choose, compelled with persistence—you will begin to establish priorities, develop self-confidence, generate enthusiasm, organize your goals, accumulate wealth, handle challenges, and continue to be the person you were meant to be. A winner!

INSTRUCTIONS

Let me encourage you to *personalize* and *internalize* these principles which have generated a turning point in the lives of many people. Read them from beginning to end, many times.

Have a pen and "highlighter" in your hand. Underline specific lines and paragraphs—a simple act that will triple your retention rate. Write your own thoughts in the margins and make it *your* book!

THE BEGINNING

Write the date you start reading this book: _____.

Many successful people in the past have traced a new, exciting, profitable chapter in their lives to the reading of a specific book. I want that to happen to you! *May the date you have just written be the beginning of incredible blessings, rewards and growth* as you BUILD YOUR OWN SUCCESSFUL AMWAY BUSINESS!

A WORD TO WISE BUILDERS

Do not mistake or misuse the information in this book. The principles offered are to serve as guides, but should not be interpreted as engraved-in-stone laws.

Moreover, as you have questions relating to this book or to building your Amway distributorship (and you will!), consult your Upline for specific information.

Dexter R. Yager, Sr.

Chapter One

Blueprints

The people in our country are the richest, freest, most powerful in today's world. How fortunate we are to be living in a land of opportunity. We can do whatever we decide as long as we do not violate the rights of others.

If my travels to various places around the world have taught me anything, that one thing would be how wonderfully blessed free people are. Millions of people in other areas of the globe would gladly exchange places with those of us who live in a free country. Most envy the opportunities we enjoy, and many would give up their families, their friends, their material possessions—all just to live in a country of unlimited opportunities.

Most people, if asked to name the greatest single benefit in life, outside of life itself, would probably say *freedom*. That desire for liberty has been one reason that many of the wars have been fought.

Yet even in the great lands of America and Canada (or any other democracy, for that matter), where everyone is politically free, most men and women are living in economic and occupational slavery—their lifestyles, hours, working conditions, vacations, and other conditions of employment are determined by someone else. Sadly, most "free" people are promoting the profits of someone else; they are building someone else's business.

Quite frankly, though some might argue, there are no *great* jobs. A person could search lists of occupations in vain, trying to find the one job which gives great opportunities and freedom to determine one's own working hours, the type of working conditions, the amount of pay, promotions, and retirement benefits. There are no jobs which offer ample amounts of *both* time and money.

Yet ideally our economic system rewards people in direct proportion to what they do. Obviously, that condition exists best when a person owns his own business within our free enterprise framework.

The free enterprise system has been called the "ultimate wealth-creating idea." In fact, the ability to create profit through private enterprise has been built entirely due to that entrepreneurial spirit.

The Amway Sales and Marketing Plan itself is a good example of what free enterprise is all about. The Plan provides an equal opportunity to all people (regardless of background, nationality, or other differences) to further their own well-being through personal effort and initiative. It's an opportunity that is not limited to those who have special skills, education, or large amounts of capital to invest. Success in Amway is possible wherever there are people in free societies who are willing to commit themselves to conscientiously build their businesses.

You have decided to build your own Amway business. Congratulations! You are joining a great, growing multitude of people who place a tremendous value upon that free enterprise system. You are becoming a part of that segment of society who believes we must continue to recognize performance and to preserve our personal freedoms (the right to own property, the right to worship as you choose, the right to express your opinions, the right to unchecked progress). In fact, you are now involved with people who believe that the freedoms we enjoy are completely tied up in the freedom to build our own business.

Liberty consists of the ability to choose. One of the great benefits of living in a free society is that we have the right to make our own important decisions. We can obey the law, or we can disobey it. (But we must then be prepared to reap the results of either decision). We can work, or we can depend on others to work for us. We can build our own business, or we can use our labors to make somebody else rich. *We* decide.

Yet with such opportunities, the large percentage of people refuse to make the decision to make things happen for themselves. Instead, they retreat to live in society's comfort zones—those stagnant places with little room for growth or potential.

I feel that one of the most foolish concepts in our world is the idea that we should all settle for mediocrity instead of striving for excellence, for reaching outstanding levels of performance, for achieving great feats, and for carving our own niches in the marketplace.

It was not always so. This nation was built by pioneers who believed in attempting great things. Our country became a major positive force in the free world because its citizens loved freedom and achievement. We advanced because we were a nation of believers and builders.

It is time that we reach for that pursuit of excellence and greatness once more. You have joined in the growing chorus of countrymen who believe in building an exciting future.

Rich DeVos, President/Amway Corporation, said the following:

I see America as the horizon of human hopes. To those who say that the design defies our abilities to complete it, I answer: To act with enthusiasm and faith is a condition of acting great.

It is time more and more of us became builders, encouragers, believers, doers, and motivators—all joined together with the common purpose of freedom.

Freedom—an abundance of time and money—must be a prime motivation for building your own business. Motivation is the inner urge which can incite you into positive action. The greatest achievements throughout history have started from that God-given urge—that dream to achieve.

But the greatest, most motivating dreams will have little lasting effect unless you determine a specific plan of action.

In the Amway business, there are certain success patterns which many men and women have already followed on their own freedom trail. This book is a compilation of those principles which have enticed scores of people into exciting, wealthy, loving, sharing business-builders.

You can be great in the world of Amway, too. You have unlimited opportunities before you. Your horizons are already stretching as far as you will allow yourself to dream.

Take advantage of your God-given dreams and freedoms. You can do the "impossible."

BUILD YOUR OWN SUCCESSFUL AMWAY BUSINESS!

BUILDING BLOCKS:

This country achieved its greatness because of small business men and women, and I'm concerned that we maintain the climate that made it possible for me and millions of others to start a business and build it.

Rich DeVos,
President/Co-Founder
Amway Corporation

Free Enterprise is so much a part of our free way of life that, when it is restricted, it is just a matter of time before other basic freedoms are threatened . . . the role of government is not to try to guarantee happiness, but to provide the opportunity for people to work out their happiness for themselves.

Jay Van Andel
Chairman of the Board/
Co-Founder
Amway Corporation

"Nowhere do habit patterns count for as much, and nowhere does the force of habit demonstrate its might more emphatically than in the business world. A businessman's habits are among the most important factors that determine whether he will be a success or a failure.

J. Paul Getty
Oil, Real Estate
and Airline Magnate

BUILDING BLOCKS:

The spirit of America is strong and its future is great! The entrepreneurs, the self-reliant, those with personal initiative, optimism and courage are leading America to take freedom's next step.

We've made a new beginning, a dramatic and far-reaching step for a much better tomorrow. We've come too far, struggled too hard, and accomplished too much, to turn back now.

We can make our beloved country the source of all the dreams and opportunities she was placed on this good earth to provide. We need only to believe in each other and in a God who has so blessed our land.

President Ronald Reagan

Free enterprise is one of the greatest blessings anyone can know. The Amway business is one of the purest forms of free enterprise. The opportunities through Amway provide unlimited potential. To me, one of the greatest breakthroughs came when I realized that if I built this business, I would never have to work for anyone else again!

Jim Agard
Amway Diamond
Direct Distributor

I truly believe that the future of this nation depends on our youth. If we teach them about free enterprise and how to dream, if we give them the love they need, and if we instill in them a confidence and pride, then we will see a better America in the years ahead.

Birdie Yager
Amway Crown
Direct Distributor

Chapter Two

Foundations

By joining the world of Amway, you have chosen to participate in one of the greatest adventures man has ever known. Let me explain.

There are several exciting books which have detailed the progress of Rich DeVos and Jay Van Andel's brainchild *(The Winner's Circle, The Possible Dream, An Uncommon Freedom* and *Promises To Keep**—all written by Charles Paul Conn). But the most important parts of this adventure are not the manufacturing plants or truck fleets or worldwide media attention.

The most exciting element in the Amway Sales and Marketing Plan is people, specifically *you*. You are the future of both our free enterprise system and the Amway business. Though it is already the most prestigious of the many multi-level marketing programs, most observers (inside and outside

---

* These items are strongly recommended and are available through your Upline. However, they are optional and not required.

the "circles") believe that Amway Corporation and its distributors worldwide are *just beginning* to see the greatest periods of growth in the history of the company.

Still, the mere mention of such terms as "Amway" or "multi-level business" draws the full gamut of emotions. Of

Amway, other multi-levels, and sex (not necessarily in that order), it has been said, "On that subject, never before have so many been so uninformed, yet were so unwilling to admit their ignorance." Everybody has an opinion, but sometimes there are few facts to back up those personal ideas.

Even today, with many Amway distributors gaining financial independence each year, there are people who still ask about the legality of the Amway Sales and Marketing Plan.

Several related terms which are being used (and abused) today:

MULTI-LEVEL MARKETING
It has been called "the Wave of the Eighties." On this point most economists agree—multi-generation merchandising is virtually exploding throughout the free world. Reportedly, in America alone, there are several companies springing up *every day*!

Already millions of people are getting involved in "pulling themselves up by the bootstraps." Such goal setting is nothing new in the corporate world. One of the major airline company presidents once started out as an operations man (baggage handler) with that same fledgling firm. Almost everyone knows of a similar success story within both neighborhood and national businesses. For those who are able to "climb the ladder" and then hang on, the accompanying social, professional, and financial rewards can be quite satisfying.

Being president of a firm of any size is a lofty goal, but for the most it is an almost elusive, impossible dream. There are many other factors besides work output which affect such top-echelon positions: political and family connections, education, the right-time/right-place factor, and friendships. Perhaps most unnerving is that, normally, there are many others waiting in the wings for a shot at the same position. A company/corporation president is allowed very few mistakes, since the stockholders can be quite unforgiving and unmerciful.

Quite frankly, very few people in the free world have the hope of reaching high corporate pinnacles. And even those who dream of owning their own business—whether it is a community grocery store, a cozy restaurant, a fast-food franchise, an auto parts store, a motel, a gas station, or hardware store—all are going to require a substantial investment of money *and* time (translation: blood, sweat, and tears) before the accountants can begin to use anything but red ink.

In fact, the Small Business Administration estimates that between 60 and 80 percent of all new businesses that begin each year will be but a tragic memory within five years. Not

only does the staggering overhead cause the downfall of so many businesses, but the starting costs of most enterprises defeat most new businesspeople even before they begin. Figure 2-1 gives you an idea of the considerable amount of money needed just to start up your own business. Obviously, beginning any business which requires such substantial up-front money can be risky at best.

FIGURE 2-1

Business	Starting Costs (x 1000)	Business	Starting Costs (x 1000)
Appliance Store	$ 44-60	Hardware	$ 51-60
Auto Parts	47-100	Ice Cream	25-70
Auto Repair	35-95	Imports	30-60
Bakery	20-50	Jewelry	50-100
Barber	15-25	Liquor	72-100
Bar, Cocktail	58-106	Men's Wear	40-95
Bookstore	40-55	Motel	175-350
Beauty Salon	10-50	Paint	25-99
Coin Laundry (44 unit)	110-130	Pants	30-80
Car Wash	60-66	Pet Shops	25-60
Camera Shop	62-100	Photo Studio	20
Crafts	30-66	Plants	11-44
Campground	35-100	Printing, Quick	29-52
Day Care	25-77	Radio - TV	40
Deli	25-90	Restaurant (medium)	50-100
Donut	25-75	Sandwich Shop	50-125
Dry Cleaner	74-100	Service Station	41-60
Electronic Shop	30-160	Shirts	25-60
Florist	37-40	Shoe Store	43-128
Furniture	46 - up	Sporting Goods	48-68
Family Clothing	61-100	Tennis Court	300
Gift Shop	27-50	Tire Dealer	35-65
Garden	27-50	Toy Shop	64-100
Grocery (small)	37-56	Travel Agency	7-30
Health Food	25-44	Tune Up	20-50

Multi-level marketing, on the other hand, offers immediate income *and* room at the top, for an unlimited number of people. Those people can come from all walks of life. The high levels of achievement depend solely upon one's own efforts in his/her individual quest for rewards and recognition.

In a capsule, the multi-level distributor is in business for himself, but *he is not by himself.* He normally buys already developed and marketable products, has the potential of selling his merchandise to retail customers, sponsors other distributors, then teaches his "downline" people to follow the wholesale product use/retail/selling/sponsoring pattern. For his efforts, he receives either a bonus or a series of bonuses from the parent company. Sponsoring, either personal or indepth, is the key factor in making that multi-generation business into a long-term success.

More importantly, as a self-employed businessperson, the multi-level entrepreneur has control of the success of his own business. He has the flexibility, freedom, and opportunity to fail or prosper. Since he owns his own business, he has no boss nor salary, though obviously his Upline has a vested interest in helping him succeed. He needs no employees nor building in which to operate (to start with, at least; and there are Amway Diamonds who still operate out of their homes), so the overhead remains minimal. And because the multi-level businessperson ideally has a number of both customer/clients and downline associates, the loss of one usually is not catastrophic, compared to the misfortune of a salaried employee who looses his entire paycheck.

The multi-level entrepreneur has an unlimited growth opportunity. Saturation never has and never will be a problem. He can enjoy legal tax deductions from operating his business. And, most importantly, it opens many doors to becoming a family operation. Both husband and wife can contribute their talents to building the business, and children can quickly become involved in the day-to-day operations of product flow and downline communication.

With all multi-level systems, *unless products move,* nobody gets paid, either immediate profit (commissions or percentage mark-ups) or bonus money, which is a major difference between multi-level marketing and pyramids (also to be discussed in this chapter). The one unalterable fact about multi-generation systems is that sales and product flow come naturally as the result of building one's own organization in width and depth. The more depth (the greater the number of added downline generations/levels), the larger and more permanent the flow of business volume for your own distributorship. And yet each new downline distributor (in the best multi-level businesses) has the *same* unlimited potential as the *first* people who got into that particular business!

Yet multi-level marketing is certainly not all that unique or mystical. It is merely product movement through a system of multiple generations of distributors and consumers. The unique part of multi-level marketing is that the gigantic sums of profit go to the distributors, not the manufacturer's representatives, the jobbers, the wholesalers, or into retail overhead.

At *worst*, it is an ingenious system which eliminates the disadvantages found in other types of businesses. At *best*, it can be an avenue toward unlimited opportunities for wealth, recognition, power, and friendships. There are over 638,000† millionaires in the U.S.A. and 20% of them made their fortune in the last six years in multi-level marketing.*

DIFFERENCES

More specifically, multi-level marketing differs in form from other, more historic methods of product movement:

*From *Business Connections*, January, 1984 and *U.S. News and World Report*, July 4, 1983.

†Presently there are approximately 1.4 million millionaires in the U.S.

DIRECT SALES: This is the oldest, most personal form of marketing. From the earliest days where one person bartered goods or services with another person, to today's polished professionals armed with their flip-chart and multi-media presentations, this form of one-to-one contact has accounted for a tremendous amount of product flow.

With this method, the salesman generally buys merchandise at wholesale (or discounted) prices, then presents his wares directly to the consumer.

From the dedicated ten-year-old who shows up at your front door with those boxes of tempting cookies, to the most suave insurance, cosmetic, and home products representatives—all are people who are employed in the often-profitable realm of direct sales.

There are inherent advantages and disadvantages with this marketing system. The latter includes the fact that with most direct sales companies, profits depend solely on one's own ability to move merchandise personally, as opposed to the geometric potential through multi-level marketing, to be discussed further. Also, when the direct salesperson decides or is forced to change areas or territories, he normally needs to start developing his clientele or consumer routes all over again without the benefit of maintaining proper contact with those previous clients/consumers.

RETAIL SALES: Every neighborhood has clothing stores, grocery markets, car dealerships, and gasoline stations; with each, the owner/manager buys products from a manufacturer/supplier at wholesale costs, and sells these products to customer/clients at retail (marked-up) prices.

This concept of marketing, of course, evolved from direct sales into the small merchandisers, then during the Nineteenth Century into general stores and department stores. Even today's sophisticated "discount" stores fall into this category.

The majority of business done around the world is through retail sales, but there can be tremendous problems with overhead, building upkeep, storage, personnel, security, etc.

The many costs involved—from manufacturers to distributors, and from wholesalers to retailers—all add up to decreased profits for the retailer and increased prices for the consumer.

A quick glance at Figure 2-2 gives some idea of where the consumer's dollar goes.*

FIGURE 2-2

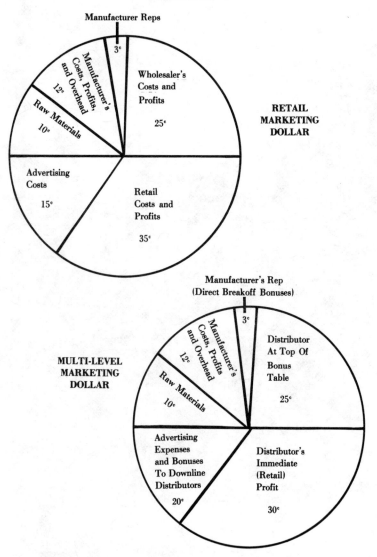

*Research used for figures was compiled from several companies. Figures are used as examples only, and not to be misinterpreted as any guarantees or specific earnings representation.

That comparison of the marketing dollar should quickly help the reader to understand why multi-level marketing is the fastest growing method of moving merchandise.

As long as there are goods and services to be exchanged for money, there will continue to be retailers in every community, but the multi-level entrepreneur espouses a simpler method of supplying merchandise to the consumer, with a distribution system which essentially cuts out the middlemen. By getting back to the basic free enterprise system, the multi-leveler can develop a higher percentage of profits and bonus for himself while delivering a better quality, more advantageously-priced product to the consumer.

MAIL ORDER: Another long-standing form of retailing is handled through those catalogs, pamphlets, and advertisements to which nearly everyone has responded.

Whether it is the Alaskan fisherman who sends his check and order to Chicago for a new pair of thermal underwear, or the Carolina housewife who requests the "amazing" 43-piece set of kitchen gadgets (all for $19.95!), mail ordering has proven to be a convenient method of obtaining merchandise.

There are some inherent problems, such as the postal and delivery system, but Americans have grown up enjoying the convenience of shopping at home—enough, at least, to put up with the week to month delay.

In fact, a few of the multi-level companies (such as Amway) have added the beneficial elements of mail ordering from catalogs, and they have ingeniously been able to maintain the profit and bonus system with at-home catalog convenience.

PYRAMIDS

Anytime the discussion of multi-level or network marketing arises, the inevitable question about pyramids

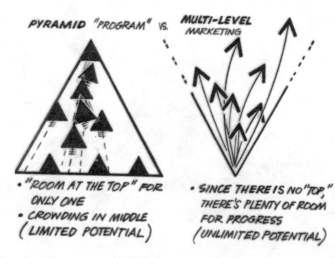

PYRAMID "PROGRAM" vs. MULTI-LEVEL MARKETING

- "ROOM AT THE TOP" FOR ONLY ONE
- CROWDING IN MIDDLE (LIMITED POTENTIAL)

- SINCE THERE IS NO "TOP," THERE'S PLENTY OF ROOM FOR PROGRESS (UNLIMITED POTENTIAL)

seems to follow. This method of "sales" or "marketing" has been confused universally with both mail-ordering and multi-leveling.

Most states have stringent anti-pyramiding statutes, yet there seems to be a never-ending succession of get-rich-quick "business networks" and chain-letter schemes. All can generally be described as requiring a fee for the opportunity to bring others into the "program," then one receives a portion of the fee "downline" associates pay for the same opportunity to bring others in.

The Federal Trade Commission has released numerous descriptions of illegal pyramid systems, including the following:

> Such schemes are characterized by the payment by participants of money to the company in return for which they receive (1) the right to sell a product and (2) the right to receive, in return for recruiting other participants into the program, rewards which are unrelated to the sale of the product to ultimate users.
>
> As is apparent, the presence of this second element, recruitment with rewards unrelated to product sales, is nothing more than an elaborate chain letter device in which individuals who pay a valuable consideration with the expectation of recouping it to some degree via recruitment, are bound to be disappointed.

One of the major differences, then, is that legitimate organizational and income growth must be based on increased product sales, rather than simple downline expansion. Unfortunately, even some companies who call themselves "multi-level" fall into this unethical category.

Another note of comparison is that such illegal pyramids and questionable schemes are built from the top down—only those who get involved in the beginning can reach the top (in terms of profit and recognition). However, with true multi-levels, each new distributor starts at "zero," but has an equal opportunity to build his own organization to an even larger scale than his own sponsor.

Some people have lumped together all multi-level systems as being this type of illegal network, but you can rest assured in the fact that the Federal Trade Commission, an arm of the U.S. Federal Government, ruled in 1979 that Amway Corporation is a legitimate multi-level business, and not a pyramid.

Therefore, anyone who still tries the "Amway is just another pyramid" argument has nothing more than eroneous personal opinion on his side—certainly not economic logic or factual information.

MULTI-LEVEL GUIDELINES

One of the most important facets of the ideal multi-level company is that its goal should be a steady, continual growth of both the distributor organization and product sales volume. "Flash in the pan" companies, on the other hand, almost always promote rewards based primarily on either recruitment, or on large initial merchandise/inventory purchase requirements.

Another test rests in the concept of maintaining a consistent, growing balance of both retail sales and sponsoring, of training (or duplicating) the new distributors in such a plan, and rewarding those who follow this balanced pattern. The key word is *duplication*.

Additionally, the Better Business Bureau (BBB), a national network of private agencies which provide consumer protection information, has published a booklet called "Tips on Multi-Level Selling Plans" (Number 239 B 25174), which lists the following protective guidelines concerning multi-level/generation businesses:

1. The basis for the company's promotion should be the retail sale of the product, not just the unending recruitment of distributors.

2. The firm should acknowledge that it is not necessarily easy to sell or recruit and train other sales people, but that it requires time, effort, and personal commitment.

3. Investors should be wary of promises of quick, high potential earnings.

4. The firms should provide national or regional advertising on a regular schedule along with the introduction and promotion of new products.

5. Distributors should be assured of a continuous supply of quality products.

6. The recruitment of additional distributors or sales personnel should be based upon the potential market, population of the specific community, or prior sales competition. Limiting the total number of distributors in a state on the basis of the entire state population may not be adequate protection for a distributor in any given community within the state.

7. The company should set standards for advertising local business opportunity meetings and also for all sales recruitment literature.

8. The company should accept the responsibility of checking the qualifications of potential distributors and remove those who violate company policies or local laws.

9. No more than a minimal initial inventory should be required to become a distributor or dealer.

10. A reliable firm should guarantee in writing that any products ordered, but not sold, will be bought back by the company within a reasonable period of time for a certain percentage of the original price.

AMWAY ADVANTAGES

A quick check of the Amway Code of Ethics/Rules of Conduct (included in your product/literature kit) will show why our supplier, Amway Corporation, is held in such high esteem by economic experts, consumer advisors, and political/social leaders!

Because of our long-term commitment to fairness and excellence, most multi-level systems admit that Amway Corporation is the premier standard for this growing industry.

Unfortunately, many have been "burned" in the multi-level realm, primarily due to inconsistent company policies often resulting in bankruptcies, poor payment processing, poor product quality, and inadequate distribution. Such tendencies are not true, of course, with all multi-levels, but many more systems have passed into oblivion than have remained.

I am *slightly* prejudiced(!), having spent over two decades receiving checks from Ada, Michigan, but I believe there are many reasons why the Amway Sales and Marketing Plan is the "Cadillac" of multi-level programs.

FACILITIES: Our phenomenal growth from a small converted gas station back in 1959 to today's modern, beautifully landscaped facilities throughout the world reflects the long-term, consistent success of our supplier, Amway Corporation.

In Michigan alone, Amway now occupies over 3,000,000 sq. ft. of office, manufacturing, research, distribution, and other support facilities.

With a growing number of corporate acquisitions, Amway's worldwide owned and leased building space is in excess of 7,500,000 sq. ft.

That doesn't even include such widespread facilities as the farm in California (where NUTRILITE® food supplements are organically grown), to the acerola cherry orchards in Puerto Rico, to the luxurious Peter Island resort, and a growing list of other related Amway-owned localities.

RESEARCH: Our supplier, Amway Corporation, owns a multi-million-dollar Research and Development Center where more than 250 scientists in 28 laboratories work to perfect the ever-expanding, 350-plus product line.

MANUFACTURING: Amway's modern, sophisticated facilities reflect a commitment to quality. Product return rates annually average *a fraction* of one percent!

DISTRIBUTION: An extensive rail, truck, and shipping system efficiently transports more than 350 million pounds of Amway-related products to over 40 countries and territories each year.

ADVERTISING: A multimedia campaign, including advertisements and television specials featuring Amway Distributors, carries messages supporting your business to millions of people on network television, radio, and in 90 million issues of leading consumer and trade magazines.

COMMUNICATIONS: The more than 3,000,000 copies of magazines and newsletters that roll off Amway presses each month, along with exclusive product and business opportunity literature and motivational audiovisuals, keep distributors and customers informed about Amway people, products, and places.

FINANCE PLAN: Showing true initiative and a constant commitment to meet the needs of today's consumer, Amway Corporation now offers the **AMWAY FINANCE PLAN.** This plan, of great benefit to distributors and their customers alike, offers financing options for all Amway® products, as well as an ordering and shipping program for these products, with no out-of-pocket expense to the distributor.

MEETINGS: Each year, more than 100 Amway-sponsored seminars, meetings, and rallies bring together product, sales, and business specialists to help you build your business.

Diamond-sponsored functions* (Weekend of the Diamonds, Go-Diamond, family reunions, Leaderships and Dream Nights, and Yager sponsored Free Enterprise Celebrations) give your distributors an added, exciting insight into: training, motivation, and the growing number of success stories.

In addition, qualifying distributors attend exclusive leadership seminars in a variety of locations: from Ada (Michigan), and Maui (Hawaii), to Burgenstock (Switzerland), and many other locations throught the world.

*These functions are strongly recommended and information is available from your Upline. However, they are optional and not required.

LEADERSHIP: Any organization rises and falls with its leaders. Amway's founders, Jay Van Andel and Rich DeVos, are the closest of friends, joint chief executive officers for the world-wide billion dollar corporation, and much-heralded leaders. In addition to being featured in such well-known publications as *Reader's Digest* and *Saturday Evening Post*, both have received such prestigious honors as the George Washington Honor Medal from the Freedoms Foundation, the Golden Plate Award from the American Academy of Achievement, and the Religious Heritage Business and Professional Leader of the Year Award.

Besides the long list of distinguished positions both have held, Van Andel has served as Director and Past

Chairman of the Board for the United States Chamber of Commerce, and DeVos was appointed Chairman of the National Congressional Leadership Council.

Both DeVos and Van Andel are leaders in their church and actively support a wide range of civic, political, and cultural interests.

Joining such able leadership is the Board of Directors of the Amway Distributor's Association, men and women who are *elected by qualified distributors from distributor ranks*. That, in itself, is an additional factor why Amway Corporation has remained a trendsetter in the multi-level systems.

The Yagers have co-hosted television shows and have been featured on such programs as CBS' 60 Minutes, Carolina Camera, PTL Club, PM Magazine and The Richard Roberts Show. They have been the subject of many newspaper and magazine articles including USA Today, Christian Life and On Magazine. Known in the business world as among the wealthy and successful, they have written several motivational books which exemplify their dedication to family, faith and achievement. Dexter has also received the 1976 Bicentennial award for the Most Outstanding Christian Businessman of the Year.

In 1985 Dexter received the Humanitarian Award for his charitable contributions. Birdie has a degree in Nutrition and Herbology.

YOUR PLACE ON THE TEAM

Business experts around the world are realizing the tremendous advantages of viable multi-level marketing companies. Estimators insist that by 1990, such systems will collectively be doing in excess of $100 billion annually! That is BIG business by anyone's standards.

More importantly, a large chunk of that amount will be merchandised through Amway distributors—people just like *you.*

By joining those ranks, you have the opportunity to be part of the winningest, most profitable marketing team in history.

For one thing, you do not have to re-invent the multi-level wheel. So many MLM professionals develop their organization around one product, then look for another product to pass down that network for increased profitability. Neither you nor I have to do that—the Amway Corporation has *its own* qualified staff of researchers, scientists, and developers to acquire new product lines. In addition, Amway stands behind each piece of merchandise with their incredible 100% fully satisfied money-back guarantee. By joining the ranks of Amway distributors, you place yourself, so to speak, under a very competent, ever-expanding umbrella. You are part of a dynamic team.

Plus, within the Amway Sales and Marketing Plan, you join a time-proven success plan. No other multi-level organization can match Amway in terms of reputation or success-building records. You have many, many people to whom you can look and say, "They made it in Amway, and so can I."

J. Paul Getty once wrote, "There are six requirements that must be included in your plan for success;" then he listed the following:

1. You must be in business for yourself;
2. You must sell a product that is in demand;
3. You must guarantee that product absolutely;
4. You must give better service than the competition;
5. You must reward those who do the work;
6. You must build your success upon the success of others.

If any multi-level company has fulfilled Getty's guidelines through the years, it has to be Amway Corporation. Our supplier, Amway Corporation, has pledged to offer an increasingly wide range of professional support services to help you build your business. Properly utilizing those services, you can become an independent, highly successful, extremely wealthy businessperson. Others have—you can too.

That's the good news. The bad news is this: unlike nearly every other level of society, as you build your Amway business, you will have no mother or teacher or boss standing over you, pushing you, pulling you, disciplining you, browbeating you, or holding the proverbial "carrot" (privileges, good grades, a paycheck, or promotion) in front of you. You are the boss. It is all up to you. That is the scary, uncomfortable, invisible bad news.

But there is more good news. As your own employer, you control your own promotions and paychecks. Perhaps that is frightening to some, but there are millions (even billions) of people behind Iron and Bamboo Curtains who would gladly give almost anything for such an opportunity.

How you fare depends upon how well you follow the blueprint (success pattern) and how well you develop all the basics. You can do it.

You can BUILD YOUR OWN
SUCCESSFUL AMWAY BUSINESS!

BUILDING BLOCKS:

Belief, *strong belief,* triggers the mind to figuring ways and means and how-to. And believing you can succeed makes others place confidence in you.
David J. Schwartz, Ph.D,
Author of *The Magic of Thinking Big*

Network marketing is exploding throughout the free world. It is a dynamic concept that offers immediate positive cash flow, incredible time-leveraging abilities, room at the top for an unlimited number of entrepreneurs, and strategic planning and development.

Why is this concept spreading so quickly? FREEDOM! The network marketing entrepreneur has control of his own success!

Ty Boyd
Businessman, TV and Radio
Personality, and Internationally-acclaimed Professional Speaker

Dex and Birdie's success pattern has been the prime ingredient in our growth. Their love and understanding have helped us to build that stronger marriage and family life that we all strive for. We have grown as individuals who are excited about our future together and our opportunity to offer the same future to many others.

Don Wilson
Amway Emerald
Direct Distributor

Success is based on imagination *plus* ambition *and* the will to work.
Thomas Edison
Inventor

The trip of a thousand miles begins with a single step.
Ancient Chinese Proverb

You cannot push anyone up the ladder of success unless he is willing to climb himself.
Andrew Carnegie
Industrialist

When you dismiss an opportunity, you miss success.
Ken Pitman
Amway Diamond
Direct Distributor
(Germany)

Genius is only the power of making continuous effort.
Conrad Hilton
Hotel Magnate

Some say Amway is a concept, others a manufacturing concern, but to us it's become a lifestyle.
Dominick Coniguliaro
Amway Emerald
Direct Distributor

Chapter Three

Dreambuilding

Building a shimmering glass-and-metal skyscraper requires much more than joining a few beams together and hiring an interior decorator. In fact, the largest, most important amounts of expense and mental output must take place in the architectural offices and muddy foundation trenches.

Just as the space shuttle *Columbia* burns up nearly all of its half-million gallons of fuel just to lift its 74 ton cargo mere inches off the launch pad, so the skyscraper construction must seem painfully slow and unrewarding before the gigantic framework finally begins to take form.

I have seen many new Amway distributors become discouraged when their initial efforts go somewhat unheralded and seem unfruitful.

When that skyscraper construction begins, it seems to take forever before it finally starts rising from the ground. No one considers *that* process ridiculous or unreasonable. The architects, contractors, and project managers realize that the necessary foundational work must be done well before the

seemingly quick above-the-ground construction starts. A blueprint and time-table are always nearby at the construction site for easy reference.

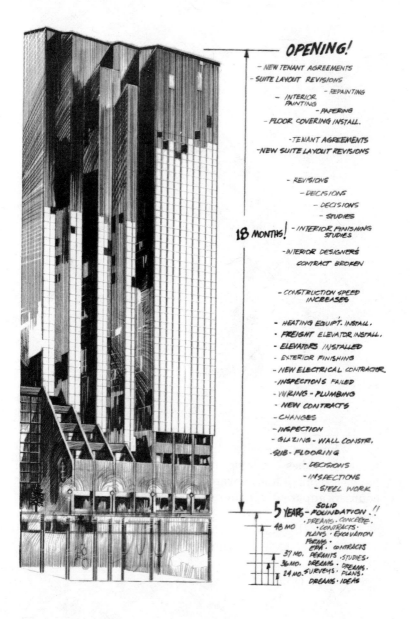

OPENING!
- NEW TENANT AGREEMENTS
- SUITE LAYOUT REVISIONS
    - REPAINTING
  - INTERIOR PAINTING
    - PAPERING
  - FLOOR COVERING INSTALL.

  - TENANT AGREEMENTS
- NEW SUITE LAYOUT REVISIONS

  - REVISIONS
    - DECISIONS
      - DECISIONS
        - STUDIES

18 MONTHS! - INTERIOR FINISHING STUDIES

  - INTERIOR DESIGNER'S CONTRACT BROKEN

  - CONSTRUCTION SPEED INCREASES

- HEATING EQUIPT. INSTALL.
- FREIGHT ELEVATOR INSTALL.
- ELEVATORS INSTALLED
- EXTERIOR FINISHING
- NEW ELECTRICAL CONTRACTOR
- INSPECTIONS FAILED
- WIRING - PLUMBING
- NEW CONTRACTS
- CHANGES
- INSPECTION
- GLAZING - WALL CONSTR.
- SUB-FLOORING
    - DECISIONS
      - INSPECTIONS
        - STEEL WORK

5 YEARS - SOLID FOUNDATION..!!
48 MO.   · DREAMS · CONCRETE ·
         · CONTRACTS ·
         PLANS · EXCAVATION
         FORMS ·
         EPA · CONTRACTS
37 MO. PERMITS · STUDIES ·
36 MO. DREAMS · DREAMS ·
24 MO. SURVEYS · PLANS ·
         DREAMS · IDEAS

51

Why then does that distributor wonder what happened when he rushes headlong into unforeseen problems? Even if he has some initial rewards, what happens when he encounters apparently monumental obstacles on his road to success?

Without the proper blueprints (goals) and dreams (the artist's rendition of that finished skyscraper), the construction contractor might become quite confused and discouraged.

Likewise, without those goals (Inner Circle, 1000 PV, 2500 PV, 4000 PV, Direct, Voting Member, Ruby, Pearl, Emerald, Diamond, etc.) and dreams (a luxurious car, the special house, an exotic vacation . . .), the Amway distributor cannot properly build his own business.

How often have you heard people say, "I just never set goals," or "I don't believe in goals. That way, I am never disappointed if I don't reach them." Such statements, while they may enjoy popularity, are pure rubbish. Everyone sets goals every day: to turn off the alarm, to get up, to eat breakfast, to go to work, to pay their bills, to watch a certain television program, to run two miles, and so forth. We have just become so accustomed to setting and reaching those everyday goals that we don't even recognize what we are doing.

What if we *didn't* set those goals? We wouldn't get up, we would starve, we would lose our jobs, and they would turn off the electricity and gas. Right?

The same thought applies to your daily, weekly, monthly, yearly, and lifetime goals. You are setting *something* as a goal, even if it is only to exist; but unless you learn to determine the proper way to set goals, you will never reach the best destinations.

Well defined and properly pursued goals/dreams direct your life. No one can set these for you, since they are a personal matter. Each must set his own goals and build toward them day by day, week by week, month by month, year by year. A strong foundation, if laid carefully and painstakingly, eventually leads to the attainment of our ideals. As in a construction project, the foundation must be strong and well-thought-out in order to allow for future planning, additions, and alterations.

DEFINING DREAMS/GOALS

Fulfillment of those dreams comes through realistic goal setting on three levels:

LONG-RANGE GOALS: If you want to build a building, you first conceptualize the entire building; you don't focus on a brick or a pane of glass. Similarly, the

Amway distributor should think BIG (Diamondship, financial independence, early retirement, time/money freedom. . .).

MEDIUM-RANGE GOALS: The contractor must consider the steps from foundation mortar to high-rise glamor. He needs to set a day by day timetable. Even though he is equally concerned with foundations *and* final decorating touches, he knows that the first floor framework must be completed before the second floor construction can begin.

The Amway distributor cannot get so concerned with going Diamond that he forgets the goals between signing the application and receiving that Diamond-encrusted pin.

SHORT-RANGE GOALS: Even the most prestigious builder of skyscrapers must still handle dirt-moving and mortar-pouring.

Short-range goals are extremely important. Unfortunately, many people ignore this category. Even those who do take the time for such details often set their short-range goals too high, so high that they become unreachable.

REALISTIC ASPIRATIONS: The fulfillment of dreams is a gradual process and needs to be worked out on a day by day basis. The establishment of immediate goals provides the stairway which eventually reaches to the fulfillment of medium and long-range goals.

But what happens when you reach the short-range goal? It should be merely the beginning of a new adventure: transform those medium-range aspirations into short-range ones; change long-term goals into medium-range ones; and then develop *new* long-term goals.

Correspondingly, those dreams which go along with each goal reward your efforts, but they must also be realistic (planning to buy a Rolls-Royce when you reach 1500 PV hardly fits the area of realism; but neither would owning a second-hand Chevrolet seem to be a fitting dream for reaching Diamond). Be realistic, but once you have reached one goal, decide to set your sights on something bigger and better. Dreams are the force that fuels you to do more and become more.

GOAL-SETTING: Success is the continual progression towards a worthwhile goal or achievement. The goals you set, then, are extremely important.

It is important to specifically define what you want, what kind of home you want, where you want to live, the kind of automobile you want to own. Just saying, "I want to own a home someday," or "I would like to have a big car someday" doesn't mean a thing. You must define the exact reason that will cause you to work toward the income you really want and need *or* a lifestyle you've always dreamed of. You must have a clear, concrete image of exactly *why* you need more income.

Especially for those immediate goals (since you learn first with the smaller ones to define the larger ones), it is important to visualize your dreams and aspirations. Write them down. Consider what you want to buy when you reach those goals. How much will that dream cost you? How soon do you want to get it? Write this information down!

Visualize your dreams and goals by posting pictures or statements in prominent places in your home and car (mirrors, refrigerator, etc.)

If one of your dreams, when you reach Direct, is to buy a new car, then get out your pen and paper. List what make and model you want. What color? Do you want velour or leather seats? Can you imagine yourself driving that shiny car up into the driveway of the friend who laughed at you for getting into Amway?

If you want a new car, go to the dealership, sit in the plush upholstery, smell the new-car aroma, turn on the stereo, drive it, and think about it until it becomes a "burn."

But don't forget, while you are dreaming, to work your business. Do everything needed to reach the goal so that you can eventually have that dream. Practice delayed gratification.

Most importantly, *don't let anybody steal your dreams.*

VISION

The necessary ingredient in the formula of success is vision—the blueprint. You will get tired. You will be weary. You will need to recharge. When those times come, you will need inspiration. Beyond inspiration, you will need great vision.

Many people are severely handicapped by short-sightedness. When someone has his eyes focused too closely on the present, the future tends to be blotted out of vision; therefore, short-sightedness is usually caused by being more interested than we should be in the immediate. That does more damage to a person's potential than anything else.

OBJECTIVES

Before we set out on any journey, we ought to know something about where we want to go, how we are going to get there, and when we expect to arrive. With tightly-held goals and clearly visualized dreams, success becomes easier. "Inch by inch, it's a cinch!"

It seems unbelievable that the majority of people spend their lives wanting to be successful, and yet, never set clear-cut daily, weekly, monthly, and yearly goals.

The saddest part is that anybody, yes, anybody—can succeed in Amway. It doesn't matter where they are presently, or where they came from, they can succeed and build a gigantic, profitable business. However, many default through negligence or neglect, and thereby choose to be losers. They start dying the moment they stop dreaming BIG dreams.

Unfortunately, most people are willing to sacrifice the future on the altar of the immediate. That universal tendency must be overcome by learning to visualize short, medium, and long-range goals/dreams.

You can do this business! You can wade through the fears and doubts and ignorance and discouragement. When the clouds of doom overshadow your vision, you can begin thinking of the advantages you will obain by not allowing yourself to become discouraged. You can think of how happy and proud your spouse and children are of you as you achieve even the smallest goals. You can image the way your heart will beat when you are introduced on stage as a new Direct Distributor, Pearl, Emerald, or Diamond! You can consider the great regard in which you will be held by others, as they realize what you have done in becoming a beacon for others to follow.

Success is pleasant only through living a life of accomplishment and achievement. Doing the things that failures refuse to do may initially seem uncomfortable, but the results will be very, very rewarding.

Napoleon once said, "I see only the objective. The obstacle *must* give way!" The great French commander always won the battles in his mind before he ever entered the field of combat. With victory visualized, the struggle means little.

So, even if you have been building your business for several weeks or months and still don't see incredible things happening, don't be discouraged. Visualize your dreams over and over. Refer to your goals. Stick to the success patterns to be presented in this book. Remember that building the skyscraper requires time-consuming foundation construction. Recall that the space shuttle *Columbia* expends most of its energy just getting that first few inches off the ground. For you, it's making that first step.

Gradually, as you follow the same guidelines which have led multitudes to Diamond and beyond, you can begin to set higher goals, reach greater aspirations, and accomplish successes you have never considered possible before.

Do It. Build your own
SUCCESSFUL AMWAY BUSINESS!

BUILDING BLOCKS:

> The heights by great men reached and kept
> Were not attained by sudden flight,
> But they, while their companions slept,
> Were toiling upward in the night.
> Henry Wadsworth Longfellow
> American Poet

Cherry:
Americans traditionally have been the most adventuresome, courageous, and successful people in all the world. We have been the pace-setters, the go-getters, the dream-seekers—the standard for the rest of the world, to strive to be the best.

Jerry:
What we are experiencing today in the Amway phenomenon is the reawakening of that heritage and understanding who we are in regards to the stock of people we come from.

The Meadows
Amway E.D.C.
Direct Distributors

Ron:

One of the greatest joys we've received is from showing the business to others who also had stopped dreaming. It has become a never-ending thrill to see the spark of belief as they see there is a way to reach their goals.

Toby:

What we are is God's gift to us, but what we become is our gift to God.

The Hales
Amway Diamond
Direct Distributors

We can easily forgive a child who is afraid of the dark; the real tragedy of life is when men are afraid of the light.
Plato

The poorest person is not the man or woman who has no money, but he who no longer has a dream.

Pat McCune
Amway Diamond
Direct Distributor
(Ireland)

Here is a fact to which there are no exceptions: we must labor for all we have, and nothing is worth possessing or offering to others which costs us nothing.

Hank Gilewicz
Amway Diamond
Direct Distributor

Chapter Four

The Geometric Multi-Level Phenomenon

Multi-level marketing succeeds when distributors share the "plan" with several people, then teach those people to share with others.

Most people new to the Amway Sales and Marketing Plan* look at the "circles" and get excited about making money, dreaming again, and possibly becoming free from the "rut system." I tell people, "It's the *dream* that you need to share." That's what incites potential distributors to action.

But when that first-night euphoria wears off, I often see negative clouds begin to form inside the new person's head

*Refer to the *Amway Sales and Marketing Brochure* (SA-4400), included in the Amway Sales Kit, for further details.

(humans naturally tend toward the negative). You can almost see the unspoken words forming: "I like everything about the plan, BUT there's just one question: How in the world am I going to use/sell enough products and sponsor enough people to ever reach 7500 PV and become one of those DD guys?"

Sometimes we who have been in the business for awhile draw the "ME-YOU-6-4-2=DD" circles casually, and forget that sponsoring 75 people, for the new couple, looks like they are going to have to gather together a vast army. On face value, those figures would be scary even to the more seasoned Amway veteran.

But the secret of multi-level marketing rests in the phenomenon of geometric progression. Let me explain.

We teach the 100 PV circles in the ME-YOU-6-4-2 format. Ideally, by the fourth generation deep, one who follows that pattern will be over 7500PV and already starting to reap the financial rewards and recognition of a Direct Distributor.

But 75 people? It seems as though it would take forever. Who even knows 75 success-oriented men and women? That's the scary part.

But remember the way the circles multiply. Just sticking by the board, you allow 6 people to come into business with you. *Everybody* knows 6, or can find them, over a selected period of time. And if you can sponsor 6, even if those 6 are less motivated than you are, they can sponsor 4. And if those 4 are only half as motivated as their sponsor, they can get 2. It's as simple as moving 100 PV or more worth of products, and you are Direct! Mathematically, it looks like this:

1 (YOU) X 100 PV = 100PV
__X 6 PERSONALLY SPONSORED DISTRIBUTORS__
6 2nd LEVEL + 1 (YOU) = 7 X 100 PV = 700 PV
__X 4__
24 3rd LEVEL + 6 2nd + 1(YOU) = 31 X 100PV = 3100PV
__X 2__
48 4th LEVEL + 24 + 6 + 1 = 79 X 100PV = 7900PV (DD!)

The system works if you work it. It is certainly not impossible. Thousands of people just like you have achieved their financial goals and dreams with those figures. Naturally, everyone isn't going to do exactly like the circles on the board. Some will sponsor more, some less.

However, before we go on, let me give another illustration which shows how exciting the geometric progression can be.

We talk about duplication a lot, and though we draw the "ME-YOU-6-4-2" circles on the board (to let everyone there know that *anyone* can work this business), such tapering off in numbers—thereby assuming that each new generation is going to be less motivated than the one previous—is not *true* duplication.

If *you* sponsor 6, then with pure duplication, *each of those people* should sponsor at least 6, and so on. Dream with me for a moment as we consider the possibilities of true duplication.

1 (YOU) X 100PV = 100PV

X 6 PERSONALLY SPONSORED DISTRIBUTORS

6 2nd LEVEL + 1 (YOU) = 7 X 100PV = 700PV

X 6

36 3rd LEVEL + 6 2nd + 1 (YOU) = 43 X 100PV = 4300PV

X 6

216 4th LEVEL + 36 + 6 + 1 = 259 X 100PV = 25,900PV

To get you to see the amazing principle at work with pure duplication, let me take it one more generation:

216

X 6

1296 5th LEVEL + 216 + 36 + 6 + 1 = 1555 X 100PV = 155,500PV!!

Let's come back to earth by saying that, in reality, you may have to sponsor 20 or more distributors to find 6 who can become motivated enough to also sponsor 6 (or even 4, as with the circles we draw), who can each then go sponsor 6 (or even 2, as with our circles), but the figures—either with the "ME-YOU-6-4-2" or the pure duplication figures can be staggering!

We teach working in depth, so you will be helping those besides the 6 (or whatever number you decide) to personally

FIRST:

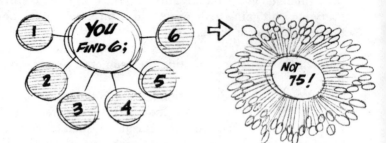

NEXT:

... HELP *THE FOUR*... EACH SPONSOR *TWO*!

sponsor. Still, to think that you personally have to accumulate and work with a vast army of "recruits" is false. All you need is 6 active distributors, and all they each need is 4 (Active distributors are actively pursuing Direct). All those third generation associates need is 2. Suddenly you could be cashing those DD checks.

As you teach the success pattern and plug those personally sponsored distributors into the motivational, self-development books, tapes, and function system*, soon they will need you less and less. You can go on to others. In fact, the fastest growing leaders generally only work with 2 or 3 "hot" personally sponsored distributors, and usually only 3 to 5 in depth under them.

The power is in the "one." It's that *next* phone call, that *next* meeting, that *next* personally sponsored associate, that *next* "warm" contact—the *next* "one" is all that matters, not the many, many calls and meetings and associates and contacts that you will have to make on your way to Diamond. It's the *next* "one" that is so important. Anybody can do just one, then one more, then one more.

It's like the old joke. "How do you eat an elephant? . . . One bite at a time."

Likewise, "How do you build your business? . . . *One* phone call, *one* meeting, *one* associate, and *one* contact at a time."

And by plugging into our success support system (books, tapes, open meetings, functions, etc.*), you can literally watch that growing network of personally sponsored and depth distributors growing, both in numbers and in business knowledge, throughout the world.

Whether your business grows in figures like those we draw on the board, or if it actually explodes more in line with pure duplication, the phenomenal power is in the geometric multiplication. Best yet, the progression comes one step at a time.

You don't have to be a miracle-worker to make this thing work, you just have to be a believer and a doer. You don't

---

* These items are strongly recommended and are available through your Upline. However, they are optional and not required.

have to be extraordinarily smart (although they will probably call you a *genius* after you reach Diamond)!

And anybody can do it. Anybody who can sponsor 6 people can also teach his downline associates to duplicate his sponsoring pattern. Anyone can use or sell 100PV of products, then teach his downline to do the same.

So there is no reason for failure with the geometric phenomenon of multi-level marketing—especially in Amway, the "Cadillac" of them all.

You can do it.

*You can BUILD YOUR OWN SUCCESSFUL
AMWAY BUSINESS!*

BUILDING BLOCKS:

Entrepreneurship, by its very nature, explains why you want to go into business for yourself. A successful entrepreneur wants to be judged on the merits of his/her own work.

Connie Agard
Amway Diamond
Direct Distributor

Owning your own Amway business is the fastest, smartest way to freedom, security, and unlimited income. Success does not just have to be an impossible dream. It's there for those who go for it!
Jerry Meadows
Amway Diamond
Direct Distributor

Far better is it to dare mighty things, to win glorious triumphs, even though checkered by failure, than to rank with those poor spirits who neither enjoy much nor suffer much, because they live in the gray twilight that knows not victory nor defeat.
Theodore Roosevelt
Twenty-sixth President of the United States

It's exciting to be able to share what we've found in this business with others. Some people get jealous of other's successes, but we never have because we have realized that we all have the same plan. Besides that, the further we go, the more we see that we've really just gotten started.
Jerry Nelson
Amway Emerald
Direct Distributor

Chapter Five

Building Blocks

If all we had to deal with were numbers and geometric progressions, this business would be a cinch. Not only *could* everybody do it, but everybody *would* do it.

Not so. We are not dealing merely with circles and marks on the board and product. To succeed in this business, we must deal with people.

People do not always follow form. They change without any apparent reason. They react negatively. They sometimes fail to see the simplest business principles.

For example, of those two couples who have seen you draw circles, Joe and Jane may be doing double-back flips and shouting, "We can do this thing! Where do I sign up? I've already written down 93 people on my prospect list while you were talking. We're gonna go Diamond!" And over in the corner, Sally has just elbowed sleeping Sam, and he sheepishly mumbles, "Did I hear you say that this was Amway?" Naturally, you look at Joe and Jane with dollar signs in your eyes, lavishing them with first night literature and a promise to make that follow-up call the next day.

As for Sam and Sally, you "recognize" them immediately as losers, and so—even though you give them the same literature and promise to call—you sigh a silent "Who cares?" as they walk out the door.

But people are funny. Just as Joe and Jane may call you up the next day and whine, "Well, we talked it over and decided not to . . . ," so Sam and Sally may be the ones who listen to the tapes, look over the literature, just "happen" to see an Amway commercial on television, or otherwise have something "click" and make them decide to build their business to Direct, Diamond and beyond.

That's just an example, but nearly everyone who has been in this business very long could tell you stories that would make the one about Joe and Jane/Sam and Sally seem quite ordinary. People are like that.

So how do you build this business? It comes by following a pattern that has helped many others become successful, wealthy, and free. It happens when you place one building block upon the next, following the architect's blueprint. Like any building contractor, you will come upon situations over which you have little control and always changing circumstances, but you must adhere to a plan if you want to succeed.

As mentioned in the previous chapter, no one can lift an entire wall in place by himself, but just as that building can be formed as you place brick after brick, then your business can be built as you geometrically enlist others to follow your pattern.

There are many such building blocks. The following are some of the most important principles you will need in building your own business. Everyone who has succeeded in Amway has traced each of those blueprint lines with his own life.

GET STARTED

It has been said that there are only two ways to fail in this business: to not get in, or to quit. That may be a quaint over-simplification, but there is much truth to it. One thing is for certain—you will never be able to cash one single Amway check unless you get started. Do it now!

READ THE LITERATURE AND BOOK, THEN LISTEN TO THE TAPES*. These first night materials are provided as a service to help you make a decision

*These items are strongly recommended and are available through your Upline. However, they are optional and not required.

about the Amway Sales and Marketing Plan. Do yourself a favor. Listen to the people who are successful in the Amway business as you decide, not those critics who "tried and failed" or the "experts" who would disparage either Amway Corporation, your line of sponsorship, or your ability to build the business.

GET BACK WITH YOUR POTENTIAL SPONSOR.
Ideally, you should see the "circles" a second time as you
further cement your decision. Count the costs, as you see
them. Are you willing to work as hard for yourself as you
are for your boss? Can you start putting aside a few
hours a week for your own business?(We never advocate
one leaving his current job until he/she is receiving Amway checks for double his/her current salary; and even
then he/she should counsel Upline).

Remember that without a dream, even in the beginning, you are like a ship without a sail. What do you
want from this business?

MAKE SOME COMMITMENTS: Once you have decided to build your own business, merely signing the application and opening that first box of S-A-8 hardly signals the impending showers of riches, recognition, and rewards. Success doesn't come in a kit; kits lack the most important ingredient: *people*. To get those people, you must first create an environment for success. Discipline is the basic foundation for building this people business, so you should get serious about your decision.

Ideally, in addition to your Amway Sales and Product Kit, you should order ten additional products (shop using your own products, not some chain-store's), several positive thinking and self-help books (ask your

Upline for a list from which to choose) and basics tapes (to help you get a quicker grasp on this business).*

Before you can excite anyone else about this fabulous opportunity, you must be excited about it yourself.

Fact: you can search the world for a business opportunity like the Amway Sales and Marketing Plan, and yet you cannot find one to match what you now have within your grasp; but until you make that commitment to the business, you will never attain the level of success you now desire.

That commitment comes through believing in your business, your goals, and yourself. Once that believability factor rises to the proper level, nothing can stop you.

That commitment should lead you to purchasing a tape recorder, a marker board (the 2' x 3' size and/or the smaller size for one-on-ones) and easel, "Decision Packs," and additional books and tapes.* All of these are what I describe as "tools of the trade." Just as a carpenter needs a hammer and nails, and just as a mechanic cannot work effectively without screwdrivers and wrenches, so you need tools to produce the proper results. You need positive information or motivational, educational and training materials to succeed. How are you going to build your own business without the proper tools?

Consistency, even from the beginning, is important. You don't build by nonchalantly slinging a few boards together and tapping once in awhile with a hammer. If you are going to do it, *do it*. If you are going to poke around, go ahead. But be honest with your sponsor by letting him know the percentage of time you can devote to building your business, so he can budget his time accordingly with the rest of his organization.

Time is your most valuable asset. Don't waste it. It is absolutely necessary that you schedule your time. Get The Schedule Book Pocket Calendar* and begin writing down the upcoming meetings and activities. Decide how much

---

*These items are strongly recommended and are available through your Upline. However, they are optional, and not required.

time you are willing to devote to *your* business and how fast you want to grow. Plan your work, then work your plan!

Remember, you either create your own environment and control your time, or someone else will.

ACTION

PROSPECT LIST: Make a list of people. Such a file, even from the beginning, is worth its weight in gold. It is your key to getting started. Don't pre-judge anyone! Don't make up a separate "chicken" list ("I'll show them the plan after I am really successful."). The biggest mistake in starting is trying to decide who would or would not be interested without even showing the plan to them.†

Your immediate prospects should include your family, friends, neighbors, fellow workers, former schoolmates, teammates, frat brothers, etc., and (quite frankly) anyone who wants to make more money and/or uses soap, etc.(!)

---

†Refer to additional prospecting literature and tapes, which are available through your Upline. However, these items are optional and not required.

Go through your address book, your Christmas card list, your school yearbooks, and names of previous job colleagues. Refer to your first night literature for additional help in developing your prospect list.

One of the most tragic mistakes new people in the business can make is to pre-judge people—to fail to list people whom they consider too busy or too successful already to need Amway. Nothing could be further from the truth. Take my word—if you want something important done quickly, find a busy person to do it. It has been said that 20% of the world's population do 80% of the work, and that the remaining 80% do the other 20% of the work.

So as you make your prospect list, look for people who are "hungry" for success (they can be broke or rich and still be hungry for more), people who want to take responsibility for themselves, and those who want to help others achieve similar successes.

The worst possible thing you can do to yourself and that prospect is to exclude him from your list merely because you pre-judged him. Many Amway distributors have done that only to see that person go across stage as a new Direct—sponsored by somebody else!

So get busy filling out your prospect list. Your sponsor will help you add to this list later, but you should start with at least 50 names. Those names may mean gold for you (literally!).

LOOKING AND ACTING THE PART: Be an actor! Wrote William Shakespeare, "All the world's a stage and all the men and women merely players: they have their exits and their entrances; and one man in his time plays many parts."

Everyone is an actor, but the majority of people act as though they believe they will not or cannot amount to much during their lifetimes.

If you want to succeed, you must act the part even before it becomes fact. When I was only 25 years old, I started building my Amway business, but there was one major problem. I stuttered. This had been an excruciating, lifelong problem for me. But I also realized that if I was ever going to be a millionaire in this business, I was going to have to start acting the part, *pretending* that I was already successful. Sure I was embarrassed and fearful, but why should I have sat around and let fear control the future?

So I began creating mental images of the person I wanted to become. I saw myself successful and talking with confidence. Then, in every situation, I tried to act and talk as though I was already that successful, confident person. As my accomplishments grew, *real* confidence took the place of the part I had been acting. Admittedly, my life wasn't changed overnight, but day by day I grew into the image I kept holding in my mind.

Stuttering may not be your problem. Perhaps you are shy or filled with "poverty thinking"; you may be "hung up" on status, or trying to overcome a lack of confidence. You know the nature of your personal obstacle, but do you know that you can *overcome* it?

Try as many of these exercises as possible for 30 days:

1. Set a goal of overcoming your insecurities and inadequacies;

2. Rehearse difficult situations before they happen (when possible);

3. Dress and look your best. A businessperson's
   clothing influences any viewer's stereotyped
   judgement of the wearer. It immediately
   establishes or destroys credibility, which is one of
   the most important qualities in any business relationship;

4. Talk constructively and positively to yourself. Focus on uplifting and constructive adjectives and adverbs. Everything you say either builds up or tears down your subconscious self-image;

5. Observe others who appear to be sure of themselves. Accept yourself as you are, but continually upgrade your own standards, lifestyle, and behavior patterns by associating with winners;

6. Concentrate on direct eye contact when you listen and respond. It is one of the most valuable, nonverbal indicators of your growing self-confidence;

7. Smile a lot! It lets people know that you are both confident and caring;

8. *Expect* success from your earnest efforts to overcome personal shortcomings;
9. Keep an ongoing list of the personal changes you have accomplished, are accomplishing, and plan to accomplish.

Remember that triumphs (especially over our own entrenched habits and fears) don't come easily, but we can become only what we expect of ourselves. We must act the part before it can become real. As Clement Stone once said, "When there is nothing to lose by trying and a great deal to gain if successful, by all means, try!"

CONTACTING AND INVITING

As you start to build your organization, you must remember that before you can sponsor anyone, you need to get them to see the "circles." Your approach, then, when you contact and invite prospects, is not to talk about Amway. Your only objective is to get them to look at a business opportunity ("I am excited, Joe, because it looks like we could make some serious money.") That's all. You should never try to explain anything over the telephone or in person ("I'd love to tell you more, Joe, but I've only got a few seconds; plus, trying to explain anything this important over the telephone would be like trying to give you a haircut through the mail!"). (Needless to say, you won't necessarily want to use this approach every time.)

Never, in talking with a prospect, should you push the name of our supplier, the products, selling, or anything to do with a part-time or husband/wife business.

Why? Are we ashamed of Amway, the products, or the concept of Network marketing? No, of course not! But I wouldn't want anyone to try to get me involved with a national hamburger franchise (a half-million dollar investment) or even in the purchase of an automobile after only a brief telephone conversation. Any smart businessperson understands that he/she needs as many facts as he/she can get and a detailed explanation of any business venture—*in person*—before he/she can make an intelligent decision about becoming involved.

Therefore, you should not tell them anything until you can explain *everything.* All you are doing is setting a business appointment. Your sponsor will conduct an opportunity meeting in your home. He will present the Amway Sales and Marketing Plan in a clear, honest, and exciting way. But he can't get your friends to your home. That is your first responsibility.

APPROACHES

There are a number of ways to contact and invite people so that they will come to your meeting (or to your *Upline's* home, an "open" opportunity meeting, or to set up an appointment at their home). In all cases, your purpose in doing the approach is to set the appointment, not to explain the business. You may wish to use a prospect tape accompanied by some literature.*

---

*These items are strongly recommended and are available through your Upline. However, they are optional, and not required.

Most of the commonly used methods of contacting and inviting fall into these few categories:

THE TELEPHONE APPROACH: This utilizes many of the other methods, but is good to start with in the business, since it allows *you* to control the time. There are a few basic guidelines concerning telephone use:

1. Practice, practice, practice! You learned to drive in the parking lot or on those backroads, not on the interstate highways; so spend time practicing into a "dead" telephone before you actually start contacting and inviting.
2. Smile before you dial. Your positive attitude shines through, even when you are only connected by telephone receivers.
3. Don't pressure people to come (it's a business opportunity, not a disease that you are trying to give away)!
4. Don't beg people to come.
5. Don't get people there under false pretenses. There is no need for deception. Just let people know, in a minute or less, that you are inviting them to hear about an exciting opportunity to make money.
6. Arouse curiosity, but don't try to explain it on the telephone. A rule of thumb: from the second you spent *more than a minute* on the telephone during an invitation, each second lessens the chance that the person will come to your meeting.
7. Let them know that there is no obligation.
8. If you will use the phrase, "I can't promise you anything," liberally during the short telephone conversation, it takes momentum away from them.

The FLOW CHART on the next page gives the possibilities for effective telephone approaches:

FLOW CHART

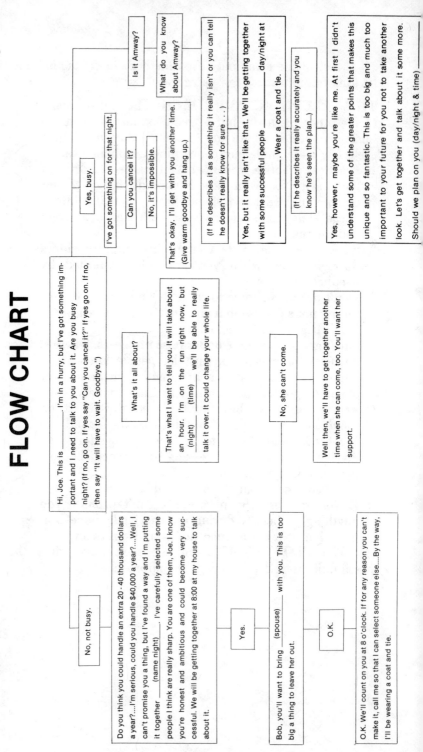

the "New Amway?"

If he/she asks, What's the difference? . . .

Plenty! Then follow through with questions he/she may not be aware of—the International business aspects, Automobiles, Travel, Legal Business, etc. Let's get together and talk about it some more. Should we plan to meet you day/night & time _____?

Is this selling?

Do you like to sell?

Yes.

Well, this could be just what you've been waiting to hear. Be over at 8 o'clock.

No.

I don't blame you. You'll love the possibilities with this business....teaching, training, counseling, traveling, helping other people, being your own boss....be over at 8:00. However, I do not want to deceive you. There will be some selling, but nothing you wouldn't enjoy. After you see the Marketing Plan, I'm confident you will agree with me.

THESE EXAMPLES ARE NOT THE ONLY ONES. THEY ARE NOT NECESSARILY THE BEST NOR EVEN THOSE WITH WHICH YOU FEEL MOST COMFORTABLE. DON'T MEMORIZE! CAPTURE THE SPIRIT OF THE WORDS!

INVITING OUTLINE — Your attitude not just the words you say, control your success in inviting. Do you have a $250 or a $1,000,000 business? Remember, you do not need any one particular person or couple. Don't beg! Generally if both husband and wife know the prospect, the man should do the inviting. The words you say in inviting should be tailored to fit your personality and your relationship with the person you are calling. However, below you will find an outline which if properly followed in sequence can steer you past most obstacles encountered in inviting by phone.

THE BEST FRIEND/CONSULTING APPROACH:
This form of contacting and inviting can probably be used only during the early phase of your business.

It takes place when you call or see a friend, and explain that you are excited about a new business venture, and that, since he/she is a successful businessperson, you would like his/her opinion. When he/she questions you, explain again that you are just getting involved, that you don't really know enough about it to explain it clearly, but that you would really like him/her to visit as your associate shares some exciting ideas.

Another version of this is when you first start showing the plan for yourself. Let your friend know that he is under no obligation, but that you are just starting to learn some important parts of your new business venture, and that you would like to share them with him to get his business opinion.

Whichever approach you use, you are complimenting your friend. Few true friends, even if they know what it is, will turn you down under those circumstances. More importantly, you are arousing his curiosity so that you can explain your plan.

THE PROFESSIONAL CURIOSITY APPROACH: This method can take many different forms, but the primary purpose is to whet that person's interest enough to come see the circles being drawn, without giving him so much information that he infers that it is Amway.

I am of the opinion that the curiosity approach, in whatever form, is the best. I am also sure that you could carry a sign around in the middle of your town: "AMWAY MEETING TONIGHT . . . ASK ME FOR DETAILS!", and eventually get someone to your meeting! The question is this: which method works best?

After all these years in the business, I still teach what I consider the best method of contacting and inviting.

Get the small talk out of the way, then say something like this: "John, have you ever considered doing something besides what you are doing now?" Most people will answer positively.* Then say, *"Listen, I can't promise anything*, but I am involved in an exciting business venture, and I feel like you are the kind of sharp person that I am looking for to make some serious money. Now, I don't have time to get into details right now, but I would like to sit down with you and show you what I've got. Check your calendar and see if you are available for Thursday evening around eight. My wife will be there.

*Be sure to properly qualify your prospect, making sure he/she is open to invest some of their time to see this opportunity. You don't want to waste their time or yours either.

Will your wife be available?" If the answer is no: "That's no problem, John. I believe it's important for her to see what we discuss, so she can aid you in your decision, so let's choose, say, Saturday evening. Is that OK? Yes? Great!"

Don't be deceptive. Let them understand that you are inviting them to a business meeting. If they ask questions, counter with question (refer again to the telephone approach FLOW CHART).*

But under no circumstances, as you approach people, should you immediately get involved in a detailed explanation of Amway or the multi-level concept. Many people have a hard enough time understanding the business when they see the circles drawn, so giving them fragments of the business, either in person or over the telephone, will only cause them to either be prejudiced against Amway or to be confused. Either way, he will protect his ego by telling you flatly that he is not interested.

There are many variations on the above approaching techniques. You can use the third-person method; "I am looking for a couple of sharp people who are interested in making some serious money. I'd like to sit down with you sometime and explain my business, then perhaps you could recommend your friends or associates to me." Or use the direct method: "I know that you have been looking for some additional income, and I would like to sit down with you sometime to share one of the most exciting ways I have found. What would extra income do for your lifestyle?"

The main point to remember is to always keep looking for dream-directed success-oriented people with whom you can share your business.

So what if a few turn you down? Trust me—there are many, many people in your community who are praying to find a way to make additional income. It is just a matter of whether *you* contact and sponsor them, or if you let someone else do it. Believe me, screening through those who don't want it, to find a few who do, is worth the effort.

---

*When expressly asked, "Is it Amway?" you should not deceive him/her in any way, but rather answer with the following as an example only: Yes, but which are you referring to, the old Amway or the "New Amway?" Then continue with the appropriate approach.

If you really believe that you have the greatest opportunity available, then the least you can do is to let your friends, family, acquaintances, and success-oriented strangers know about it. They can judge the Amway Sales and Marketing presentation for themselves. If your belief level isn't that high yet, then you need to listen to more tapes, read more books, and attend more functions.*

You can learn to make the right kind of contacts. I believe in you. Your Upline believes in you. Don't get "cold feet" over a few simple rejections.

You can do it.

You can BUILD YOUR OWN SUCCESSFUL AMWAY BUSINESS!

---

*These items are strongly recommended and are available through your Upline. However, they are optional, and not required.

BUILDING BLOCKS:

All personal achievement starts in the mind of the individual. Your personal achievement starts in your mind. The first step is to know exactly what your problem, goal, or desire is. If you're not clear about this, then write it down, and rewrite it until the words express precisely what you are after.

Every disadvantage has an equivalent advantage—if you'll take the trouble to find it. Learn to do that and you'll *kick the stuffing out of adversity every time!*
W. Clement Stone
Author of *The Success System That Never Fails*

When we realize that we are utilizing only a very small percentage of our potential, that thought can drive us past any fear, and it can propel us forward to the attainment of our goals! Unlimited abilities, coupled with a proper attitude toward others, brings *action*. Action causes success. There are no limitations to the mind except those we acknowledge.
Jack Reid
Amway Diamond
Direct Distributor

Knowing what our goal is and desiring to reach it doesn't bring us closer to it. Doing something does!
Dan Williams
Amway Crown
Ambassador

The tragedy of mankind is not this or that calamity, but the waste of man's potential for greatness.
William Ellery Channing
Nineteenth Century Boston Clergyman

Happiness is found in *doing*, not merely in *possessing*.
Tim Bryan
Amway Diamond
Direct Distributor

The hardest victory is the victory over self.
Aristotle
Philosopher

People are as happy as they decide to be. If one wants to be happy, he must think happy and act happy. If he wants to be successful, he must act successful. If he wants to be liked, he must like. The way we think determines the way we are viewed by others, so people's responses to us essentially come from ourselves.
Fred Harteis
Amway Double Diamond
Direct Distributor

Success is not measured by the heights one attains, but by the obstacles one overcomes in their attainment.
Booker T. Washington
Inventor and Educator

The future belongs to the believers.
Doris Pitman
Amway Diamond
Direct Distributor
(Germany)

Chapter Six

Construction

Let's move to that first meeting. It is very important to you and your business. Its importance places more value on the approaches you are learning to make.

Concerning that first meeting, it is also important to remember why those people would consider giving up an evening in front of the television to come listen about your business opportunity.

Why would they come? Obviously there are few people who—honestly—would not like to make more money. Most people feel that they are overtaxed, underpaid, overrun by inflation, and insecure about a down-scaled lifestyle in the future. Everybody, when they are candid, knows about those problems, but it is up to you, or you and your sponsor, to offer hope to them.

Therefore, *the attitude you carry into that meeting, even the first one, has an added dimension of importance.*

FIRST MEETING

Ideally, your sponsor will show the plan for you, but it's up to you to get the people into the living room. We recommend that you do the following:

1. Set a definite night for the meeting with your sponsor.
2. Invite *twice as many people* as you think will come, since some people may have last-minute conflicts or hindrances.

3. Set up the meeting room comfortably and put extra chairs out of sight. Bring them in only as needed.
4. Place the marker board opposite from the entrance of the room.
5. Do not have children or pets in the meeting room. If anyone shows up with either, your sponsor's wife or your wife should promptly take them to another area of the house and plan on babysitting while the meeting takes place.
6. If you are a man, wear a tie with your dress shirt, and a coat, and pay particular attention to shining your shoes. If you are a woman, wear a dress or skirt and blouse; this is a business meeting, and proper dress is critical, even if only your next-door neighbors are coming.

7. Plan to serve refreshments after the meeting or when the speaker designates, and always keep the treats simple (Active 8® Drink, NUTRILITE™ Food Bars, other NUTRILITE products, and coffee).

CONDUCTING THE MEETING

Begin on time: Don't wait for latecomers (15-20 minutes is okay for social conversation). If someone is late or doesn't show up, don't mention that to those who are there. The ones who are there are the only ones who are important during the next hour. They should feel like they were the only couple invited.

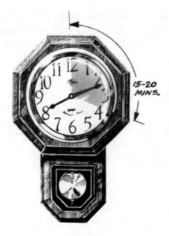

The host of the meeting (which is you, if the meeting is in your home), should introduce the speaker, who may be your sponsor. Use a few short phases, such as the following (written out on a card if you are unsure of yourself): "My wife and I are just getting started in a fantastic business. We are very excited because a friend and business associate, Joe Jones, has offered to come and explain the opportunity to you. We're going to build this business, and we would love to have you join us. Joe?"

Take notes and record the meeting. After 2 or 3 such presentations, you will want to start presenting the plan yourself.

Be excited! You and your wife should be the most interested people in the room. Don't interrupt the speaker, but show your belief. If you have questions, save them until after the meeting.

THE MEETING FORMAT

Your sponsor will use his own style of presentation, but he will always use the following format (as you will, too):

1. The introduction of the speaker by the host (2 minutes);
2. He will set the new prospects at ease (2 minutes);
3. Dream session: talk about goals and the importance of setting those into a specific time-frame. Paint a picture of the dreams the person can have when he reaches his goals. Unless the people have a dream, or can get one, then they don't need the plan to be presented (10-15 minutes);
4. 2-5 year plan and a comparison to the 45 year "rut" plan (8-10 minutes);
5. The marketing plan (15 minutes);
6. History of Amway Corporation (5 minutes);

7. Line of sponsorship (5 minutes);
8. Product demonstrations: 2 or 3 at the most (10 minutes);
9. Wrap-up and end dream session (5-10 minutes).†

CLOSING THE MEETING

During the refreshment break, the hostess should have everybody serve themselves. Don't serve them. This will get everyone mixing together.

Generally, those who are interested will ask you or your sponsor questions. Listen to the way your sponsor answers. Questions do not indicate antagonism or disbelief. They signal a desire to know more.

Set the next meeting while your sponsor and your prospects are together. Ask your prospect, "We've been drinking coffee at our house tonight; how about if tomorrow night we drink some coffee at your house so that we can both get another look at this business?" Or, "There is another get-together at my sponsor's house Friday night . . . Jane and I can pick you and Sally up at 7:30 . . . Is that time okay for you?"

You want them to leave excited about seeing the circles again. You also want them to leave with the idea of urgency—that *now* is the time to build for their future!

Perhaps one of the most important things you do during the entire first meeting is to lend them the First Night Opportunity Pak* (which is suggested by our organization). Many people, unmoved by the presentation, catch a dream while listening to the tapes, or reading the literature in that Pak.

---

†We recommend introducing the *Amway Sales and Marketing Brochure* (SA-4400) at this time. (All prospects must be given one.)

*These items are strongly recommended and are available through your Upline. However, they are optional and not required.

Also, it is good to send a few products home with them to try, and possibly include a copy of the *Profiles of Success*. Point to a few pictures and share an anecdote or two from the stories in that book.

Most of all, before they leave, let them know that you are excited about building the business *together with them*.

FOLLOW THROUGH

If a follow through is important in tennis, golf, and basketball, it makes sense that it is even more crucial in this business, and it begins during that first meeting.

You need to set up a follow-up meeting with the prospect who has just seen the circles, preferably within 24-48 hours, during the peak time of excitement. Ideally, this has already been set up during the close of the first meeting.

A simple telephone call can reconfirm the follow up meeting. You should either stop by their house (to pick up the Pak if they definitely aren't interested) to take them additional literature or tapes*, or to take them to another meeting (you want them to be around more successful Amway people as soon as possible).

Be prepared. Do not ask, "Are you getting in?" or "What have you decided?" Assume that they are ready to get started.

Rather, you should ask questions that cannot be answered with "yes" or "no"—such as, "Joe, how many names have you already started putting in those circles?" Another good question to ask is this: "Dave, what did you like best about the business opportunity?" Or try this one: "After seeing the circles and having some of your questions answered, would Tuesday or Friday be best for you to have a get-together in your home and get some good things started for you?"

Always set up two meetings. One might be an open meeting for follow through, and one or more should be in their own home.

Regardless of their decision, you should view every person who sees the plan as one of the following:

1. A DISTRIBUTOR: An associate who is going to build the business with you;
2. A CUSTOMER/CLIENT: Even if he doesn't want to get started right now, he can get started on some basic Amway products, then—who knows?
3. ONE WHO GIVES REFERRALS: If he doesn't want to build the business himself, ask if he knows

---

*These items are strongly recommended and are available through your Upline. However, they are optional and not required.

anyone who might be interested in making extra income. Again, who knows? He might even reconsider.

HOLDING YOUR OWN MEETINGS

Any motivated person will soon see that his business will not grow until he "gets on the board" for himself. Your sponsor will undoubtedly be glad to continue showing the plan for you, but his time is limited. If you are serious, you must begin to draw the circles as quickly as possible.

Study the marketing plan, but don't get "hung up" on trying to be perfect before you even try (or you may never start). Make notes. Listen to several different people present the plan, if possible.

Then practice giving the opportunity plan aloud. Get used to hearing your voice going through the format over and over again. Sure, you will make mistakes (both in practice and during meetings), but everyone does!

Just before you are ready, if possible, draw the circles for your sponsor. Take his criticism.

Prepare well. Any good speech begins with an introduction, has an identifiable body, and ends with a strong conclusion. So it should be with your plan.

Gain and hold attention by being natural and real, by setting an atmosphere that is condusive to listening, by looking your best, by establishing your authority from the beginning, by speaking to the needs of your audience, through audience involvement (questions—especially during the dream session), by using humor, and through keeping your voice lively and loud enough to be heard by everyone in the room.

In additon, use terms familiar to your audience (don't speak "down" to an audience, and neither should you "snow" them—be yourself).

Finally, respect time limitations. If your audience finishes before you do, you have failed. Quite frankly, *the most important part*, especially the first time your prospect sees the circles, *is the dream*. Get that couple dreaming enough to get into the First Night Opportunity Pak. The dream, the literature, and the tapes sponsor more people than a lengthy discourse detailing everything down to the last statistic. Your job, more than anything, is to get that man and woman dreaming!

NOBODY IS PERFECT

One of the hardest facts to face is that some of your closest friends and family will (a) laugh at you; (b) not get in business with you; (c) freely dump horror story after horror story about Aunt Margaret—"She got in that thing and lost thousands of dollars," or a neighbor—"She says that soap puts holes in your clothes," or . . ; (d) wonder why you, with such a wonderful, status-filled job, would want to do "that Amway thing;" or (e) all of the above.

As hard as it is to understand or believe, not everyone will be happy with your choice to build your own business. We shouldn't isolate that merely to Amway, since not everyone was ecstatic with your other decisions to improve yourself either. (Your college degree, or that new position which required you to move across the nation, or that new car, or even joining that tennis club.) People simply don't like change, in themselves or in others.

Plus, many people are not ambitious enough to want this opportunity. When you realize this, you will eliminate some of the heartache and disappointments that will undoubtedly be part of your growth on the way to Diamond.

Not everyone is going to come to hear the opportunity (the Diamond is where he is because he has had more "no-shows" than you have).

Not everyone who sees the circles is going to get into the business (despite the incredibly fantastic job you do showing the plan!). People naturally tend toward the negative. As a Crown Direct Distributor, I still have people look at me, eyeball to eyeball, and say flatly, "It won't work." Unbelievable!

So? What are you going to do if all your family and friends laugh at your dreams? You either quit, or you get gutsy and decide to prove them wrong!

Discouragement and lack of persistence are the two greatest enemies you will face. Determine, from the beginning, that you will stare them down and go on. The rewards at the other end are too exciting to let a few "stubbed toes" keep you from realizing your dreams and goals.

Perhaps this will help get the proverbial monkey off your back: once you have shared the opportunity with someone and have helped those you sponsor to the limit of your knowledge, ability, and time—then it's up to them to pick up the ball and run with it.

Just remember, it is much easier to build the business fast, rather than wallowing around the mundane ruts which others want to drag you into.

One of the greatest (and perhaps scariest) parts of this business is that you set your own pace. You make it happen. You get out of your business what you put into it.

So work smart! Give your time to all the people you sponsor, but *concentrate* on those who ask questions, who "chase" you, who follow the success system, who are excited about building their own business.

One final point: Don't ever call up a new distributor and talk solely about how much he is selling. That negates the positive part of multi-level marketing. We don't downplay the importance of retailing, but we don't push selling. Permanence comes through emphasizing sponsoring and building.

When you ask them about the retailing part of their business, it makes them wonder about your motives. ("Did he sponsor me just so I can move products, or is he genuinely interested in helping me build my business big?")

Additionally, when you telephone downline people, let them feel that you are sincerely wanting to help them, not merely "checking up" on them. We are not in *direct sales*. We are in a *multi-level business*. We should always be aware of the difference.

Sure, there are many details—many building blocks—on your way to constructing a massive Amway business.

Not once in this book have I said it would be easy—just worth it!

Keep remembering that you can have anything in the world that you want when you help enough other people to reach their goals and obtain their dreams.

It takes organization, dedication, perspiration, and anticipation. But you can do it.

You can BUILD YOUR OWN SUCCESSFUL AMWAY BUSINESS!

BUILDING BLOCKS:

It is not the critic who counts, not the man who points out how the strong man stumbled, or where the doer of deeds could have done them better.

The credit belongs to the man who is actually in the arena; whose face is marred by dust and sweat and blood; who strives valiantly; who errs and comes short again and again; who knows the great enthusiasms, the great devotions; who spends himself in a worthy cause; who, at the best, knows in the end the triumph of high achievement; and who, at the worst, if he fails, at least fails while daring greatly.

Theodore Roosevelt
Twenty-sixth President
of the United States

The person who wins success is the one who makes hay from the grass that grows under the other person's feet, and who doesn't restrict his efforts to the hours when the sun shines.

Unknown
Quoted from
the *Reader's Digest*

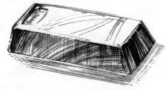

We make our own decisions in life. We are not totally helpless. We determine our own direction! Success takes work and faith.

Birdie Yager
Amway Crown
Direct Distributor

Chapter Seven
Additions

We may or may not like to be called salespeople, but in Amway, as with any effective multi-level marketing system, there is selling involved.

In Amway, we have so many products that the bulk of your sales may initially be to yourself, but there is no reason why you cannot also begin to retail merchandise to customers.

To know how to sell your AMWAY® products, you must first *know* those products. This one factor is the major reason for ordering several new products each week. You are simply replacing negative (!) merchandise, but you are also becoming familiar with and excited about your own line of products. You must know the advantages of your merchandise, as compared to the disadvantages of the competition, before you can become proficient at explaining the selling features.

Amway continues to do a thorough job of providing you with product information. Your job is to convert that raw knowledge into understanding the benefits which your customers can enjoy through the products you sell.

There are several major reasons people buy anything: pride in the benefits of whatever you are selling (such as cleaner clothes), economic advantages by buying your product (which you can easily show by explaining Amway's concentrated merchandise), protection of one's self and loved ones (which explains why so many people are experiencing tremendous profitability through selling AMWAY® home improvement, health and fitness, and security items), love and acceptance (better health of one's family), and comfort (which you can provide through conscientious service). To sell, you must build on these.

While it is true that financial freedom in Amway comes through building a large organization (in depth and width) rather than through retail sales, there should be a balance. Organizational growth helps keep your business expanding, but the retail sales throughout that organization can fuel tremendous excitement (it is hard to get discouraged when you are making a lot of immediate income *and* sponsoring new people).

If you, personally, would develop ten regular retail customers, it could increase your monthly profits by approximately ten times, since each family uses approximately the same amont of products that you use in your home; they will either use Brand X or the AMWAY® products you sell to them. Now, multiply that profitability times the number of people in your organization. Imagine if each of them developed ten new retail customers!

Especially with such high PV and immediate profit items as the AMGARD® security systems, QUEEN™ cookware sets, and water treatment systems, it just makes good sense to retail a growing volume of products.

MARKETING

While this book is not a primer on all the products which Amway distributors can make available to their customers, it is an attempt to remind you of the most important and basic factors in making a sale.

First, when you sit down with that prospective customer,

remember certain points, but stay away from a memorized speech.

Next, it is important that you let them know from the beginning that you are interested in them as people, not merely as consumers. Ice-breaking small-talk should center on them, their children, things they are interested in, and their needs. Ask questions. Listen.

Once you establish a rapport, use what you learned from the questions to your advantage. Together, determine your client's needs. Ask them about specific cleaning problems or make-up preferences. If you are attempting to sell an AMGARD® Alarm system, let them share certain fears or security factors that concern them. You can talk about *your* interests and get nowhere, but when you let them express *their* needs, you are well on your way toward making that sale.

Once you sense and determine that person's needs, it is up to you to show how your products can meet those needs. You must quickly focus your attention upon the benefits, advantages, uses, and money-saving features of your merchandise. This is where your own belief and product knowledge makes the difference. Demonstrate those products. Provide proof for your claims.

Develop the *need* into a *want*. She may need the products you are showing, but until you change that need into a want, you will probably not make the sale. Use as many of the human senses as possible. Help that person visualize the benefits. Don't sell products, sell delicious tastes (as with NUTRILITE™ food supplements and drink mixes), aromatic smells (colognes), beautiful sights (ARTISTRY® jewelry), and attention-getting sounds (AMGARD® Alarm systems). Sell health, not NUTRILITE® vitamins or water treatment systems. You get the picture, don't you?

Then make the transaction. Practice handling the money questions. Visualize your customer signing that check. Don't be afraid to ask for money. Remember that Amway's 100% money-back guarantee is even better than a free sample because the customer's satisfaction is based upon using the entire product, not just a small amount.

Answer any questions which the client may have. Pinpoint any objections which may come up in the conversation (which are usually just questions for more information, not real objections).

Don't make the mistakes of talking your client out of buying because of your own feelings of inadequacy as a salesperson. Continue to visualize the transaction taking place. Form this mental picture: you carried your friend's products over from your home, and now your friend has your money in his pocket!

Then build on that sale. Establish the client as a regular customer. Ask for referrals. If that person enjoys certain products, she won't be able to keep quiet. When they talk about their new "find" to others, you can quickly add new clients to your list.

Before long, you can even suggest to your original client that those referrals could be their customers, then proceed with setting up an appointment to show the Amway Sales and Marketing Plan to them!

Above all, be consistent. Establish 10 to 20 regular customers. Service them at least twice a month. Your retailing will become an effective, money-making factor as you

BUILD YOUR OWN SUCCESSFUL AMWAY BUSINESS!

BUILDING BLOCKS:

I will greet this day with love in my heart.
For this is the greatest secret of success in all ventures. Muscle can split a shield and even destroy life but only the unseen power of love can open the hearts of men and until I master this art I will remain no more than a peddler in the market place. I will make love my greatest weapon and none on whom I call can defend against its force.

My reasoning they may counter; my speech they may distrust; my apparel they may disapprove; my face they may reject; and even my bargains may cause them suspicion; yet my love will melt all hearts liken to the sun whose rays soften the coldest day.

Og Mandino
From his book,
The Greatest Salesman
in the World

The root of motivation is faith. Faith and motivation are interchangeable parts of the synchronized machine of success . . . and they can work for anyone who chooses to apply the success principles tempered with faith and motivation.

Jim Kinsler
Amway Diamond
Direct Distributor

Chapter Eight
Cement

Franklin D. Roosevelt once said, "It has always seemed to me that the best symbol of common sense was the bridge."

If you would be both a success and a leader, you must learn to creatively build bridges in all of your relationships with people. Such important elements are a unique part of our business, and the things which build lasting relationships are the cement which holds your growing business together.

WIDTH AND DEPTH

I have been writing to you about building width in your organization of profitability and depth for long-term security. Those phrases should become imprinted in your mind.

Still, there are some myths and misconceptions about building your business with width and depth. For starters, some think that they have to know thousands of people to develop a gigantic organization. That just isn't true. Even though you may have thousands of distributors in your organization even by the fourth downline generation (as discussed in Chapter Four), *you will primarily be working*

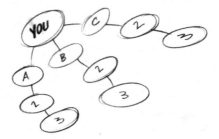

with three wide and three deep at a time, not thousands. No one could work effectively with that many people.

The key is duplication. We say that building your Amway business boils down to teachers teaching teachers to teach. There is more truth to that than any of us know.

One of the myths concerning duplication is that by sponsoring a person, you have just duplicated yourself. Nothing could be further from the truth. You have not effectively duplicated yourself until that new person is becoming successful at sponsoring, moving products, and teaching. That takes time and effort. Without that effort, you have merely sponsored an "orphan," and your business will not see much volume or growth coming from that distributor.

Ideally, we teach sponsoring "legs," not just individuals. To do this, you must first develop leaders, then you must back up your leaders with leaders (teachers teaching teachers to teach—remember?). The leader may not be your frontline distributor, but may come in depth; still, you must back up that leader with another leader.

Now, you can go out, sponsor lots of frontline distributors, move a lot of products, and call yourself a multi-level marketing genius; however, *until you are growing in depth, you are merely involved in direct sales.* Your income still depends directly upon your month-to-month efforts, not on a growing organization.

Width without depth will prove temporary. You will inevitably encounter "salesman burnout" on the part of your distributors. That's why you need to work depth. Depth brings security.

When you are building in depth, the income will almost always be two to three months behind your growth. In other words, you may not reap the profits from working downline nearly as quickly as with frontline sales. You must understand that you are building the foundation for a lifelong business. Keep working width and depth—in balance—don't be discouraged if you aren't reaping incredible financial rewards during the first months. Keep sponsoring. Keep retailing. Keep working downline.

You will obviously have to learn to budget your time as more and more people begin to come into your organization. As mentioned, you should ideally work three legs wide at a time until they are three levels deep, but it never works out quite that way. Sometimes you have to work wider than that, and often you have to work much deeper holding meetings. You have to slow down for some distributors, speed up for some, and let others stay "on the back burner" for awhile.

How do you know where to spend that valuable commodity called time? What are some signals to look for in the people who will become leaders?

First, look for that person who "chases" you. He will hound you sometimes, asking lots of questions about sponsoring, buying a board and easel, and holding meetings. That's one of the first signs of a leader.

Also, a leader will inevitably start "parroting" things he has heard or read from the tapes and books. A person who quickly gets immersed in positive materials is a learner and a leader, not a leaner.

A leader will be excited about the products, wanting to learn more about them—how to use certain items, and how to merchandise them most effectively.

You will notice that a leader will take notes. He will write down goals and dreams. He will eagerly show you a good prospect list. You don't have to brow-beat a leader into doing those simple things.

A leader is somebody who is either positive or quickly learning to be that way. It is an excellent signal when he constantly goes out of his way to build up people and the business rather than finding fault. That type of person is simply more fun to be with. He will attract others to himself—inside and outside of the business.

A leader will seek to be around you and other successful people in the business. He will be at the meetings and functions. He will be there with or without a new prospect. And he will still be asking questions.

When you find leaders with these traits, spend time with them. Don't ignore others who are less motivated, but you should always "fan the fire." Teach those who are most willing to be taught. Your time is money, so utilize it to the fullest by working smart, building both depth and width, and by looking for leaders. Don't just sponsor distributors—build legs.

BUILDING LEADERSHIP
It's probably very obvious by the time you have reached this far in the book, that multi-level marketing (and more specifically, Amway) is slightly different from the large corporations. In the corporate world, you attain higher and better paid positions through stepping over, around, and on people as you climb to the top.

In this business, however, you cannot build anything worthwhile, nor can you attain higher levels, unless you are willing to teach others everything you know. You succeed best when you duplicate yourself. The better your downline distributors do, the more profitable your business becomes.

However, as the leader in your organization, there are several similarities to the corporate world. You must know your business. You must be willing to take risks with people. You cannot lead your organization by merely brow-beating your downline associates.

EXAMPLE
You lead through example when you want downline growth. If you want your people to listen to more tapes, then you start listening to more. If you want your people to stop nit-picking, then take a good look at the words and attitudes you have been exhibiting. If you want your downline men and women to retail either AMGARD Alarm systems or water

treatment systems, then you must get out and set the standard.

If you have some deadheaded people who don't want to sponsor or retail, then let them see you out sponsoring and retailing with new people.

Somehow your people will know if you are being hypocritical about any portion of this business. They will automatically pick up on your negative points. Don't expect your downline associates to do something that you aren't doing.

If you are to be an example, you must keep your people in tune with what's happening in the business. Some of them won't bother to check their calendar to see that a seminar and rally is coming up. They may have forgotten about an opportunity meeting in their area.

And, as an example, it is important that you get them around other Amway people. Excitement breeds excitement. One of the most important elements in the Amway business is the sense of belonging to the most exciting organization in the world.

Get them to the major functions. Make sure they are making new friendships with other distributors.* Be certain that they are recognized and awarded for each new level. Make the business theirs.

Isn't that why people go to sporting events and motion pictures when they can stay at home and watch the same things on television? It is the event—the happening. People want to be part of something that is challenging, rewarding, and exciting.

As you lead by example and get your organization involved in the world of Amway, they will duplicate what you are doing with their downline people.

One of the hardest parts of setting an example is that you must continually grow to stay ahead of the leaders charging behind you. But, believe me, when you are getting new pins and seeing them receive new pins at the same time, the rewards are worth the struggle.

LOYALTY

The dictionary defines loyalty as follows: "to be constant and faithful in any relationship, employing trust or confidence."

Elbert Hubbard wrote, "If you work for a company, in heaven's name work for it."

---

*Avoid discussing or planning specific business related subjects with distributors in other organizations than yours, as this is known as Crosslining and is a violation of the Amway Code of Ethics.

As an employee, be the best worker in your company. Especially when you get in Amway, you should be an example of loyalty (plus, it will really make them miss you when you do "get free" and leave someday soon). Don't ever make calls or do Amway-related activities on your boss's time. Not only is it dishonest, it sheds a bad light on all Amway distributors.

Likewise, if you are going to work for yourself (on your own time, of course), then work for yourself. Loyalty to Amway Corporation, to your business associates, to your church, to your nation, to God. It's very important. Without loyalty there is little progress.

Not that there aren't reasons to find fault with everything around us, but as Teddy Roosevelt once quipped, "One man in the arena is worth ten, a hundred, a thousand harping critics."

Negativity and disloyalty seem to go hand and hand. One who is either negative or disloyal is always eliminated in success' race.

Conversely, superloyalty is the greatest mark of a leader. To be a success in this business, you would do well to seek that character strength. Since you have already undertaken the task of building this business, you should commit allegiance to it.

Your loyalty makes you radiate enthusiasm. It lights up your entire personality, puts a sparkle in your eyes, and money in your pocket (try it and see if it doesn't work that way, too). In fact, loyalty is a far greater incentive than money.

EDIFICATION

Listen to almost all of the tapes or talk to anyone building this business, and the term "edification" will inevitably be heard. Why?

Like loyalty, edification creates the best environment for growth. Let's face it, we live in the "me" age in a society that places little emphasis on the team concept. For most, one of the most refreshing parts of joining the Amway "team" is starting to hear people being built up.

Edification has to start in the home. Amazing things can happen in your business when you begin learning to complement and encourage your spouse and children instead of

criticizing and blaming them. When you, as members of the same family, understand the necessity of building on each other's strengths and overlooking those weaknesses, you are well on your way to getting it together, together!

The next form of edification is towards your upline. That kind of dedication may require you to do what is being taught without even understanding why, but it only makes sense to realize that your upline has your best interests in mind. He would be foolish to hinder your growth, especially since his business can't grow unless yours prospers. You don't have to always agree with your upline, and neither do you have to believe that he is perfect, but why discuss those disagreements and beliefs with anyone? Saying the negative creates doubt. Doubt causes confusion. Confusion stops growth. Lack of growth causes failure and fear. Why not replace those negatives with *faith*. Faith, after all, is the essence of edification.

Edification of your downline is also extremely important. Verbalize encouragement: "Joe, you've got what it takes to build this business . . . you are great at dealing with people." Few Diamonds would have made it without encouragement and edification, especially at those critical moments when the voice inside them was screaming, "I can't do it! I don't have what it takes!" Often your people will build their business on the pure strength of your belief in them, even when they don't believe in themselves yet! Plus, when they see you edifying both your upline and downline, they will naturally follow the pattern.

Edification is one of the most important ingredients to duplicate throughout your business!

FRIENDSHIP

It has been said, "When you build a friendship, you build a distributorship." It is true. I can say that, since I have seen it happen to lots of people who have become quite successful in the world of Amway.

But it goes beyond mere distributorships. In fact, one of the most wonderful parts of this business is the relationships you will form through the years.

In our mobile society of impermanence, one by-product has been the loss of lasting relationships. For many coming into this business, one of the most shocking, disturbing realizations comes at finding out one's lack of true friends. When they laugh at you, try to discourage you, or fail to believe in you—they lose the term "friend" by default.

You have a chance to make a difference. When you make contacts for your business, seek first to be a friend. When your new distributor has his/her first "no-show" ("me-show"), and has just found out that not all his/her pals are friends, you are the one who has the power to build or destroy, through *your friendship*.

There are many ways to nourish friendships. Permit people to be themselves—imperfections and all. Don't feel threatened if their opinions and tastes sometimes differ from yours.

Listen a lot. There are millions of books sold each year on speaking, but the most effective method of developing relationships and effective communication is through caring enough to listen. Verbalize to your friends what you like about them and how thankful you are for their presence in your life. Delight in their talents and applaud their successes.

Be honest. Open communication is the essence of friendship, so it is okay to express your feelings on occasion. However, there is a tactful way of even disagreeing. Of course, it is wise to be aware that, at times, some things are better left unsaid.

Treat your friends as equals. In true friendship, there is no Number One, no room for showing off how smart and successful you are, no room for envy, nor for feeling either superior or inferior.

Trust your friends and associates. We live in a messy, imperfect world which is made up of imperfect people. Trust, despite imperfections, is essential to building lasting relationships.

And be willing to take risks. One of the obstacles to developing close relationships is the fear of rejection and being hurt. A person cannot build his Amway business without being vulnerable, but unless we dare to love others, we condemn ourselves to a sterile, unsuccessful life.

"Do unto others as you would have them do unto you"—it's the Golden Rule by which we strive to build our businesses in the world of Amway, but that rule is also the great mirror which truly reflects the thoughts, acts, and ambitions of every individual.

Without loyalty, without edification, without friendships—all by-products of the Golden Rule—you cannot build a successful distributorship.

Those traits are the cement bonding all the building blocks together. But you can develop the kind of character it takes. You can be loyal. You have what it takes to edify your spouse, your family, your upline, your downline associates. You can nourish friendships. Sure, there are risks, but what are the alternatives?

You have unlimited potential. You can do it.

You can BUILD YOUR OWN
SUCCESSFUL AMWAY BUSINESS!

BUILDING BLOCKS:

Hal:
    This is a lonely world without people to experience the great times with. There's no way successes or fame can replace the close friendships we've found through this Amway business.

Susan:
    When it comes down to it, success isn't measured by how much money or possessions one accumulates, but by the true friendships developed.
The Gooches
Amway Diamond
Direct Distributors

So long as we love, we serve; so long as we are loved by others I would almost say that we are indispensable; and no man is useless while he has a friend.
Robert Louis Stevenson
Author of
Treasure Island

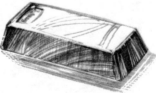

You can make more friends in two months by becoming interested in other people than you can in two years by trying to get other people interested in you.

Dale Carnegie
Author of
How to Win Friends and Influence People

Success comes, I believe, when you are finally able to take your eyes off yourself and begin to see others' needs and wants. It's been said many times, but it has never been truer: if you help enough other people achieve success, you *will* be successful and you *will* reach your own goals.

Hona Childers
Amway Diamond
Direct Distributor

Once we got involved in the Amway business, and once we saw the dream of financial freedom, we never questioned the fact that we *would* build this business.

The knowledge that some of our friends wouldn't or couldn't see the dream just made our "burn" get hotter—to show them, to prove to them that we had made the right decision.

Billy Florence
Amway Diamond
Direct Distributor

Stay consistent . . . be persistent . . . and you will achieve your goals! Consistency and persistence are two of the greatest "secrets" for success.

Donna Stewart
Amway Diamond
Direct Distributor

Chapter Nine

Better Buildings

Some years ago, a researcher decided to find the secret of success. After months of study and countless interviews, he finally gave up. "There is no secret," he said, "it is all related to hard work. One must climb the ladder to success, not just be lifted on an elevator."

Thomas Edison, chagrined when people related his success to chance, said: "I never did anything worth doing by accident, nor did any of my inventions come by accident."

Even the great Michelangelo pointed out, "If people knew how hard I work to get my mastery, it wouldn't seem too wonderful after all."

So it is with anything worthwhile, especially your Amway business.

It takes work to make progress-checks, to tabulate your organization as it exists and what you want it to be each month; to counsel upline about your progress; to counsel downline distributors concerning their efforts; to set new goals; to maintain a sense of urgency in both sponsoring and retailing. That takes much more perspiration than inspiration.

It takes great effort to teach the pattern for success—to first learn, then teach, then teach the teachers to teach. *But the plan only works if you work it.*

There are, however, ways to work smart.

THOUGHTS

Thinking is the basic process to becoming successful and building your Diamondship. What you achieve in this business (or in life) is a direct result of what you think, so it is important to develop right mental attitudes. Thinking wrong, believing wrong, and confessing wrong always leads to an unhappy, unprofitable way of life. Don't take that direction.

To think success, to become better, and to believe big, you must develop the right kind of mental processes.

David J. Schwartz, Ph.D., in his book, *The Magic of Thinking Big*, wrote the following:

"Persons who reach the top rungs in business management, selling, engineering, religious work, writing, acting, and in every other pursuit get there by following conscientiously and continuously a *plan for self-development and growth.*"

Likewise, Ralph Cordiner, Chairman of the Board of the General Electric Company, said this to a leadership conference:

". . . We need from every man who aspires to leadership—for himself and his company—a determination to undertake a personal program of self-development. Nobody is going to *order* a man to develop . . . Whether a man lags behind or moves ahead in his speciality is a matter of personal application. This is something which takes time, work, and sacrifice. Nobody can do it for you."

You have been programmed to be negative, to disbelieve, to be skeptical. But you can change. Those negative experiences, the minuses—these can be transformed into positives and pluses simply by changing your attitudes.

William James said, "The greatest discovery of my generation is that men can change their circumstances by changing their attitude of mind."

We teach changing those thoughts by changing the input. What goes in must come out. You control the future because you have the power to control your thoughts.

Some say success is just a decision away. That is true, on the surface. But that decision must be backed up with solid effort.

You are in a business with tremendous, unequaled opportunities. Your growth potential, return on your investment, reward for your efforts, and personal independence are limited only by your vision and desire (in short, *your thoughts!*).

So be enthusiastic! You have a lot to be excited about. Verbalize that excitement to yourself in the mirror, to your family, to your associates. Remember, all of us are actors.

Be positive! You should develop a habit of reading positive mental attitude books the first thing in the morning, during the day when possible, and the last thing before going to bed. The list of available materials is almost unending: *The Bible, The Magic of Thinking Big, Acres of Diamonds, How to Win Friends and Influence People, Believe, The Go-Getter,* anything by Og Mandino, Dale Carnegie, Robert Schuller, J. Paul Getty, Norman Vincent Peale, Paul Conn (concerning Amway) and of course the growing list of books authored by Birdie or myself.* Ask your Upline for suggestions.

Be learning! The tapes available to you through your upline are your personal education. Welcome to "Amway University!". You have the opportunity to have your choice of successful distributors and/or business people to ride along with you and teach you how to build your own business.

Be involved! You become like the people with whom you surround yourself. Why not with success-oriented persons? Just as the hottest, glowing chunk of burning coal quickly becomes a dying ember when separated from the furnace, so you destroy your own "burn" when you avoid the rallies, open meetings, training sessions, seminars, and weekend functions which are available to you. Being with other positive Amway

---

*These items are strongly recommended and are available through your Upline. However, they are optional, and not required.

associates helps you and your downline people to see the big picture. It builds your faith in the success system when you see it working for so many others. You must associate with positive people to build this business.

Be sponsoring and working in depth! "Now, what does that have to do with positive mental attitudes?" you ask. You may have heard the phrase, "Nothing succeeds like success." It applies to your business. Reading books, listening to tapes, and going to meetings are all necessary motivations, but their value is diminished unless you see results in your business. However, when you sponsor your six distributors, then you help each of them sponsor their four, then those four their two, it excites and motivates everybody up and down the lines of sponsorship. If you doubt this, call your own upline and tell him you just sponsored four new people in last night's meeting! And if your downline goes out and sponsors several "hot" distributors in depth, *you cannot help but get excited.* New blood always breeds excitement, especially when those checks keep getting bigger!

Observe yourself very closely, as soon as you begin developing positive mental attitudes and mastering the principles of success. Your financial status will begin to improve, and everything you touch will become an asset to you. Success comes to those who become success conscious. That happens when you control your thoughts through the proper input.

WINNING

A winning attitude is vital. People want to associate with winners.

Merely knowing the difference between winners and losers can help put a ton of gold in your pockets:

A winner respects those who are superior and tries to learn something from them; a loser resents those who are superior and rationalizes their achievements away;

A winner says, "Let's find a way," while a loser whines, "I don't think there is a way.";

A winner cuts through a problem; a loser tries to go around it;

A winner shows he's sorry by making up for his mistake; a loser may say, "I'm sorry," but he often does the same thing again;

A winner works harder, yet usually has more time, while a loser is always "too busy" to do the necessary things for success;

A winner is not afraid of losing, but a loser is often secretly afraid of winning;

A winner makes commitments; a loser makes empty promises.†

More importantly, winners refuse to pin the blame on others for personal failures. They share the credit for successes. They look for solutions, not excuses. They are less concerned with status than with accomplishment. They listen to the best advice, but they make decisions based on their own authority and character. Winners want the accomplishment, not just the goal; they have earned the prize not just to receive it.

And most importantly, winners realize that the difference between winning and losing often comes down to the decision, when no one seems to care, when beset by impossible odds, when a winner refuses to quit.

Anyone who saw *Rocky II* remembers the tense scene when the bloody, battered character played by Sylvester Stallone looks over at his shimmering adversary, Apollo Creed, and grunts to his manager, *"I ain't goin' down no more!"*

What will it take to make you quit the Amway business? Will you quit because you are afraid to dial the telephone, or talk in front of a group of potential distributors, or when a respected "friend" laughs at you? Will that moment come at 2 A.M. as you speed toward home on a deserted highway after traveling several hundred miles for a "no-show"? Will you quit when nothing seems to be working, and when no one, not even your spouse, believes that you have what it takes to "do that Amway thing"?

What will make the difference? What will keep you from quitting? All that stored up positive input—*that* will make the difference! The developing friendships and relationships within the business will keep you from surrendering your dream of freedom.

---

†From the book, *Winners and Losers* by Sydney J. Harris.

But there is one more factor that no one can measure. It is that invisible ingredient that no one can define. It is that unexplainable gutsy element that just won't let *you* quit when most others would give up. You will be faced with those moments, and only then will you find out whether you have the ultimate courage to win.

Increase your odds through building the strongest, gutsiest, most positive mental attitude. Fortify your inner strengths by putting in the proper patterns.

I believe you can be a strong, positive Amway winner! You can do it.

You can BUILD YOUR OWN SUCCESSFUL AMWAY BUSINESS!

BUILDING BLOCKS:

The biggest lesson I have ever learned is the stupendous importance of what we think. If I knew what you think, I would know what you are, for your thoughts make you what you are. By changing our thoughts, we can change our lives.
Dale Carnegie
Author of
The Quick and Easy Way to Effective Speaking

We believe that in America, it is our obligation to be as productive as possible. We totally believe in the free enterprise system. Our own credibility depends upon what we've done, what we are doing, and what we plan to do. We believe we can help change the world for good!
Bill Childers
Amway Diamond
Direct Distributor

The intelligent person is one who has learned how to choose wisely and therefore has a sense of values, a purpose in life and a sense of direction.
J. Martin Klotsche

Chapter Ten
New Horizons

Life does not always grant your first wish. So many fail because their first efforts miscarry; they lose heart and quit.

We must learn that obstacles are in our way to strengthen us. When we misunderstand their purpose and allow them to breed discouragement—that is, when we cannot tell the difference between temporary setbacks and permanent failure—then we want to turn off our effort and surrender our dreams.

It is necessary, as you build your own business, that you encounter hindrances and unavoidable problems. We call them "challenges". In fact, you will develop faster after you understand the value of opposition. You will get a chance to learn what you are made of.

You will get tired building your business, but don't worry about that. Weariness does not come so much from overwork as from a lack of interest in what you are doing. With your dream always flaming, you may get tired, but never weary from boredom.

So exert those business-building muscles. The strongest oak tree in the forest is not the one that is protected from the storms and hidden from the sun, but the one which stands in the open where it must struggle for its very existence against the winds and rains and scorching sun.

Effort and struggle—mental, physical, and spiritual— are the way by which we achieve. Success is not a comfort zone; it is a journey, a conquest, a series of challenges to be mastered.

As you build your own business, there are some construction constants which will help you succeed more quickly:

LEARN FROM EXPERIENCE: If you are unable to be taught by the past, you will be condemned to repeat it.

BE A DOER: Successful people are usually already doing things others are still talking about.

LOOK FOR OPPORTUNITIES: Most people pass the best opportunities by because those rough diamonds aren't cut down to size or sparkling.

AIM HIGH: Your goals make the difference between aimless wandering and effective action, especially in the Amway business.

CONCENTRATE ON PRODUCTIVE EFFORT: Most people spend the majority of time on relieving tension and on busy-work; you will become a Diamond not just because of your efforts, but because of your *effective* efforts.

KEEP MOVING: Continually set new goals and dreams for yourself; determine to be bigger and better. A lot of people are depending upon your actions.

No one else has a great a stake in your future and your family's future as you do.

By joining the world of Amway, you have linked yourself to a fantastic team. Rich DeVos and Jay Van Andel are as excited about the business today as they were back in 1959! And for good reason—it's a lot more profitable for everyone involved! The Amway Corporation is a one-of-a-kind enterprise, focusing on developing high-use, top quality products for you to use, to retail, and to promote in your organization.

You are able to tap into an upline/downline network of positive input (tapes, books, and other support material) and business-building meetings such as opportunity meetings, seminars, rallies, and other important functions.* It is a support system which has spread all over the globe.

You have the tools, the opportunity, the challenge, and the availability to build one of the most exciting and profitable multi-level organizations in the world!

You can do it, but that is no longer the issue. The most pressing question is not "Can you?" but "Will you?"

You can do it, but will you?

Will you BUILD YOUR OWN SUCCESSFUL AMWAY BUSINESS?

---

*These items are strongly recommended and are available through your Upline. However, they are optional and not required.

BUILDING BLOCKS:

Every day of our lives, we're telling our own futures. For it is what we think about, consciously and unconsciously, that becomes our compass, guiding us unrelentingly toward the destiny we have chosen for ourselves.

Earl Nightingale
Author, Speaker

The greatest elements in the Amway business are the *unseen things* . . . being with confident and successful people, learning from winners, seeing dreams come true, and being free.

No dollar value can be placed on these unseen things!

Peggy Florence
Amway Diamond
Direct Distributor

The price of greatness is responsibility.
Winston Churchill

There is so much potential in the Amway business. Once anyone begins to see how unlimited the possibilities are in network marketing, that person also becomes unlimited.

If we owe our success to anything, it is this: we treated our distributorship like a big business even when we only had a few people involved. We saw the potential. We stayed plugged into the tapes and books. We are just a product of the Yager pattern, and very thankful to be part of it!

Ken Stewart
Amway Diamond
Direct Distributor

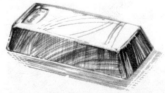

We have a tendency as humans to do just the opposite of what is best for us. Whether it's work, children, or our relationship with God, it's as if people seem bent on self-destruction. So few really get their acts together. But we saw people in the Amway business who had their personal, home and business acts together. It turned our heads around.

Don Held
Amway Diamond
Direct Distributor

Our greatest glory consists not in never failing, but in rising every time we do fail. All of history's great leaders have learned that failure is only the opportunity to begin again—more intelligently.

Dave McCune
Amway Diamond
Direct Distributor
(Ireland)

Being a success in life is not easy because life is not easy, and no rule of success will work if you don't.

Tony Renard
Amway Diamond
Direct Distributor

BEST SELLING BOOKS
By Dexter and Birdie Yager

Don't Let Anybody Steal Your Dream
by Dexter Yager with Douglas Wead

This classic in the field of motivational writing has sold more than a million copies, and is selling as well today as it did in 1978 when it was first published. Dexter Yager has influenced millions with his forthright honesty, compassion and desire to see others succeed. Here is a man who has "made it" in all the right ways, and who is willing to pour out the ideas that make for successful living.

Paperback: $3.95
Hardback: $6.95

Tales of the Super Rich!
by Dexter Yager and Doug Wead

This is the ultimate dream book! If you've forgotten how to dream, this will get you started on the road to rainbows.

- To conduct Beethoven after supper with an ivory-and-diamond baton, Baron Alfred Rothschild kept an entire symphony orchestra on call.

- The granddaughter of old Commodore Cornelius Vanderbilt loved purple. She invariably dressed in a lavender dress, carried a bunch of hothouse violets, and motored about in a silver-and-violet Rolls Royce.

- During the Spanish-American War, Mrs. Jay Gould sent the United States a $100,000 bank draft to use "anyway you can to get this war over and our boys home!" Not content with merely influencing politics, Mrs. Gould single-handedly turned one of her elegant homes into a hospital for returning injured soldiers.

- To celebrate the story-book wedding of Prince Ranier, Aristotle Onassis showered Monaco with thousands of red carnations, gave Princess Grace an exquisite diamond necklace, and donated one million francs to one of the Prince's favorite charities. It was said to have been a most satisfactory wedding gift.

Paperback: $4.95

Becoming Rich
by Dexter Yager and Doug Wead

Inspirational and moving stories of some of the world's greatest people, and the eleven principles behind their success. Stories include: Walt Disney, Albert Einstein, Martin Luther King, Andrew Carnegie, Adoph Ochs, Jackie Robinson, Thomas Edison, Helen Keller, Harry Truman, Coco Chanel, Winston Churchill, Arturo Toscanini and Douglas MacArthur.

Paperback: $4.95

The Secret of Living is Giving.
by Birdie Yager with Gloria Wead

Birdie Yager, wife of one of America's most famous and powerful businessmen, talks about:
- Marriage: How to make it work.
- Attitude: The way to popularity and self-esteem.
- Your Husband: How to make him rich!
- Children: When to say no, and when to say yes.
- Health and Beauty: They are result of our decisions, and are not automatic.
- Money: When it is bad; when it can be wonderful.
- Faith in God: Why you must deal with your guilt and inferiority, or self-destruct.

Paperback: $3.95

The Magic Makers: How to be Successful with People and Money.
Compiled by Dexter Yager and Doug Wead

Seventeen of America's leading businessmen and women share their secrets for success and happiness.

Learn how to: turn your dreams into profit; save money and invest it wisely; improve your marriage; gain the respect of your children; develop quality friendships; find faith and allow it to bring you happiness.

Included are sections from: Fred and Linda Harteis, Jerry and Cherry Meadows; Theron and Darlene Nelson, Jim and Bev Kinsler, Jack and Debbie Kronz, Jim and Connie Agard, Bill and Hona Childers, Tony and Sue Renard, Ron and Toby Hale, Hal and Susan Gooch, Gary and Diane Reasons, Bob and Kay Goshen, Jack and Effie Reid, Bob and Irene Bolin, Hank and Alicia Gilewicz, Jerry and Barb Nelson and Fred and Pat Setzer.

Paperback: $4.95

Millionaire Mentality
by Dexter Yager with Doug Wead

At last! A book on financial responsibility by one of America's financial wizards, Dexter Yager! Dexter gives freely of his remarkable business acumen, teaching you how to take inventory and plan for financial independence.

Here is a common sense, down-to-earth book about investments, shopping, advice about credit and car buying, and budgeting of time and money. Included are anecdotes about other successful American business people, to give you ideas about where to go from here!

If you are serious about financial planning, this is the book for you!

Paperback: $4.95

Available from your distributor, local bookstore or write to:
Freedom Distributing Company
P.O. Box 1110
Pineville, NC 28134
